THEMES
for early years

KT-430-521

HOMES

CHRIS HEALD

THEMES
for early years

Author Chris Heald

Editor Irene Goodacre

Series designer Lynne Joesbury

Designer Sue Stockbridge

Illustrations Claire James, Graham-Cameron Illustration

Cover based on an illustration by Sue Coney

Action Rhymes, Poems and Stories compiled by Jill Bennett

Songs compiled by Peter Morrell

Assemblies chapter by Lesley Prior

Designed using Aldus Pagemaker
Processed by Scholastic Ltd, Leamington Spa

Published by Scholastic Ltd, Villiers House, Clarendon Avenue, Leamington Spa, Warwickshire CV32 5PR

© 1995 Scholastic Ltd Text © 1995 Chris Heald
6 7 8 9   8 9 0 1 2 3 4

The publishers gratefully acknowledge permission to reproduce the following copyright material:
© 1995 Clive Barnwell for 'At the supermarket'; © 1995 Ann Bryant for 'The three bears' house' and 'Working away'; June Epstein, June Factor, Gwendda Mckay and Dorothy Rickards (editors) for 'I live up there' by Jane Bradley and 'Window in the sky' by Anita Lucas from *Big Dipper* (1980 Oxford University Press); © 1995 John Foster for 'The mouse in the attic'; © Jean Gilbert for 'In bed' and 'Who's in the garden?'; © 1995 Ian R. Henderson-Begg for 'Look around the world'; © 1995 Wes Magee for 'Washing the car'; © 1992 Tony Mitton for 'Kitchen chorus', 'My jumper', 'Sea bed', 'The lamp is on' and 'Who's been sleeping...?'; © 1993 Tony Mitton for 'Empty cottage' and 'My den' from *Conkers* compiled by John Foster (1993, Oxford University Press); © 1995 Tony Mitton for 'Home'; © 1995 Peter Morrell for 'Don't touch' and 'My friend's house'; © 1995 Judith Nicholls for 'Light the fire!'; Random House UK Limited for 'Gran's new home' from *What Shall We Do Today* by Delphine Evans (1985, Hutchinson Children's Books); Reed Consumer Books for 'Goodbye, hedgehogs' from *Winter on Small Street* by Geraldine Kaye (1990, Methuen Children's Books), 'Strange bumps' from *Owl at Home* by Arnold Lobel (1975, World's Work).
Every effort has been made to trace copyright holders and the publishers apologise for any inadvertent omissions.

British Library Cataloguing-in-Publication Data A catalogue record for this book is available from the British Library.

ISBN 0-590-53349-5

The right of Chris Heald to be identified as the Author of this work has been asserted by her in accordance with the Copyright, Designs and Patents Act 1988.

CONTENTS

INTRODUCTION

HOMES

Home is a very important place for young children. At home they feel safe, and have their own parts to play in the life of their family. The rules of home are well known, and children feel secure in knowing what to do. At home they can relax, try out different modes of behaviour to see which ones get the desired response from the adults around them, and generally try to assert their right to be treated as important individuals.

A home is not only a human need; other animals feel a basic urge to find shelter and make a nest to provide warmth, comfort and security. Children too need comfort and security before they can start to understand or learn about the world.

Young children relate best to things which affect them directly; their interest is completely centred on themselves, and it is only by using a topic which relates to their experience that an adult can hope to capture their interest and help them to learn.

The theme of Homes relates clearly to a child's experience; every child has a home to talk about and compare with others, a real situation which is encountered every day. Children will call upon their experience when playing in the role-play corner, building with LEGO, or constructing jigsaws. They will repeat situations they have dealt with at home, and react in different ways at different times, according to their mood.

AIMS

This book aims to provide adults who work with young children with a comprehensive self-contained package based around the popular early years theme of Homes. The activities have been designed for use with mixed-ability groups of pre-school and infant school age (three–six). Each activity is related to an area of the National Curriculum and deals with the early skills needed by these young children.

The topic is explored from several angles, all of which are important for the younger child. The various activities encourage the children to think about the people at home, things that happen at home, other types of homes and the wider community.

HOW TO USE THIS BOOK

Themes for Early Years: Homes is one of a series of books which has been written for adults who work with young children at home, in playgroups, in nurseries or in Infant classes.

Working with young children is rewarding, interesting and exhausting. Children are very active and need lots of adult input to keep them occupied.

The activities undertaken with these very young people need to be interesting, stimulating and age-appropriate; otherwise children will simply get up and walk away to find something else to do which they *can* understand.

Adults who work with young children need to be able to work at the child's level, realising where experience is limited and providing any support the child needs.

Young children learn best by taking part in activities which demonstrate whatever you want them to learn. They develop their understanding through real experiences such as playing with sand

and water, baking and making visits to interesting places.

Children are constantly questioning and need a supportive adult to explain many of the things they see happening in the world. Adults must try to provide answers which the child will understand.

TOPIC WEB

On pages 8 and 9 you will find a diagram of all the subject areas of the National Curriculum and the Scottish 5–14 National Guidelines covered in this book. It shows which activities are aimed at early English, maths and science, and also which activities will extend the child's experience in history, geography, technology, art, music, PE and RE. This diagram is called a Topic Web, since it enables an adult to weave together the activities he or she is going to use to enlarge the child's experience in any particular area. It is a very useful aid when planning for a block of time such as a week, a month or a term.

ACTIVITY PAGES

These pages provide a range of activities; some are original, while others give a new twist to a familiar idea. Each activity lists the resources required and recommends an appropriate group size.

Treat this book in much the same way as a recipe book – throw in your own special touches and ingredients where you feel these are appropriate, to suit the children in your group and their level of understanding.

DISPLAY

The display chapter provides a range of general information on creating stimulating displays of the children's work. In addition more detailed display ideas are given which relate to two specific activities.

ASSEMBLIES

This chapter offers a number of suggestions for assemblies or other group sharing-times. The various ideas are all linked to the theme of Homes.

RESOURCES SECTION

The photocopiable material in this book (the Topic Web, resources chapters and activity sheets) has been made available for any purchaser of the book to copy freely without the need for a licence. It is

also possible to enlarge the sheets from A4 to A3 size since, generally speaking, the younger the child is, the larger the pictures on the sheet should be.

It can often take a long time to search out suitable poems and stories relating to your chosen theme. Some resources have been mentioned in the activity pages and form part of the activity, while others are provided as additional resources for story-time and can be used at odd moments of the day. The materials in the photocopiable resources section have been specially chosen to relate to the topic of Homes and provide a selection of quality poems, stories and songs.

PHOTOCOPIABLE ACTIVITY SHEETS

The eight photocopiable activity sheets act as an integral part of some activities, and as a follow-up for others. They are suitable for use by young children, although children of nursery age will need a supportive adult close at hand for encouragement and discussion of what is to be done.

Planning towards the National Curriculum and the Scottish 5–14 National Guidelines

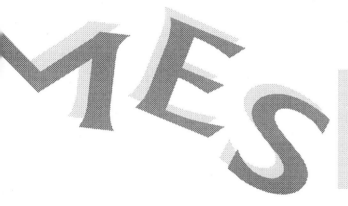

PREPARING FOR PRIMARY SCHOOL

THE NATIONAL CURRICULUM

The National Curriculum has been established to make sure that every school in the country teaches the same subjects at a range of levels. It is intended that a child will be able to go to school anywhere in the country and find the same areas of the curriculum being covered for the same amount of time every week. These subjects are: English Language, Mathematics, Science, History, Geography, Design and Technology, Information Technology, RE, Art, Music and PE.

There is a great deal of learning to be done before starting the work of the National Curriculum. For instance, before children learn to recognise words, they should understand that the written word relates to everyday speech, and they should realise that shapes and colours can be the same or different.

Young children learn best if encouraged to use all their senses in their play. They also need lots of time for free play with selected toys and materials and should, in fact, spend time on this rather than working in the traditional school manner.

TOWARDS LEVEL ONE

Children do not start on the National Curriculum until they are five, so the Programmes of Study were written to suit the maturity of children who have reached their fifth birthday and, depending on

where in the country they live, have had anything from a term to a year in school in the Reception class.

The National Curriculum provides a Programme of Study for each subject, and asks teachers to assess the level of attainment of each child in the country when they reach Year Two, partly by the use of nationwide tests, but mostly by using their professional judgement to allocate an overall level to each child.

The National Curriculum has not changed the way young children learn. A successful educator will always start with the ability level of the individual child and work towards the next step in his or her intellectual development.

THE SCOTTISH 5–14 NATIONAL GUIDELINES

In Scotland, there are National Guidelines for schools on what should be taught to children between the ages of five and fourteen.

These National Guidelines are divided into six main curriculum areas: English language, Mathematics, Environmental studies, Expressive arts, Religious and moral education, and lastly Personal and social development.

Within these main areas further subjects are found; for example, 'Expressive arts' includes art and design, drama, music and PE. Strands are also identified within each subject, for example, Maths includes problem-solving and enquiry and shape, position and movement.

Most nurseries and playgroups will find that the experiences they are offering children will be providing a good foundation for this curriculum. The activities in this book have been specially written to prepare for many aspects of it, and they will also fit well into the pre-five curriculum guidelines issued by local authorities throughout Scotland.

The activities have been organised into separate areas of the curriculum in the Topic Web on pages 8 and 9 to help you with your planning. The children's personal and social development is an ongoing theme that is incorporated throughout the activities in the book.

CHAPTER 1
MY HOME

This chapter provides activities which centre on each child's home: what goes to make a house, the furniture found in our homes and the people who live there.

FRONT DOORS

Objective

Maths — To help children recognise and order numbers from 1 to 6. This activity can also help with recognising odd and even numbers to 6.

Group size

Any size group, but ideally six to ten.

What you need

The opportunity to take children out to look at front doors in the local area (optional).

Copies of the activity sheet on page 88, the poem 'At my front door' (page 70), sheets of A4 and A2 paper, felt-tipped pens, crayons or paints, scissors.

Preparation

Arrange for parents and other members of staff to accompany you and the children, to improve the adult:child ratio. Go for a walk around the area before you take the children, to discover where there is a clear view of front doors with striking similarities and differences.

Ensure you have enough photocopies of page 88 to give a copy to every child, plus a few spares for accidents with the scissors. Establish that the children know the sequence of numbers 1 to 6 and can recognise the symbols.

What to do

Take your group of children to look at the front doors you have previously found. Talk about the materials used and the different styles of door they can see. When you return to base, sit the children on the carpet area and say the rhyme 'At my front door'.

Give each child a large piece of paper and ask them to paint the whole sheet to look like their own front door. This is often more successful if left to the next day, as children will go home and look at their own front doors. When these paintings are finished, they make an effective display if mounted next to one another with folded labels underneath. On the outside of the label write 'Whose Door?' and on the inside write the child's name. This makes an active display for a room or corridor, and provokes much conversation among passing children.

Use the activity sheet to check that the children recognise the number-symbols. The group could be asked to colour door number 1 red, number 2 blue, and so on.

Discussion

Encourage the children to talk about their own front door at home. What colour is it? What number does it have on it? Has it got a letter-box?

Follow-up activities

✧ Colour and cut out the doors on the activity sheet, then sort them into odd and even numbers.
✧ Stick the doors on to two pages of a book or a folded piece of paper, with odd numbers on one side and even numbers on the other, as in the street.

PEOPLE WHO LIVE IN MY HOME

Objective

English — To encourage the children to read the names of the people who live in their homes.

Group size

Various.

What you need

Sheets of paper and stapler to make them into a book **or** large exercise books with light-coloured covers and blank pages, felt-tipped pens, crayons, pencils, labels made of white card or stiff paper, a black marker pen.

Preparation

Cut each exercise book into the shape of a house, leaving the spine as the roof-ridge. Ensure that the staples holding the book together are not cut away, or the book will fall to bits!

What to do

Show the children the books shaped like houses, and ask them to decorate the front and the back to look like a home.

Ask the children to draw someone who lives in their home on the first page of the book. As each person is drawn, write his or her name on the page (an adult may do this if the child cannot). If the child can copy adult writing, the adult helper should write the names for the child to copy.

Once the book is completed, the child should be encouraged to read it aloud to the group (give the child individual attention and support at this stage), and the book can then be left in the book corner to be shared by the author and any other interested child.

Discussion

Talk about homes and the people who live there. (Take care, if you are in an area with lots of single-parent families, not to cause distress by assuming that children live with Mum and Dad.) Ask the children for the names of people who live with them, then they can tell you about absent fathers or mothers if they wish.

Follow-up activities

✧ Older or more advanced children may be able to think up a sentence to describe each person in their homes.

✧ Photographs can be used instead of drawings for children with special needs who need to concentrate on one thing at a time.

✧ Read 'Gran's new home' on page 75. Who has a Gran who lives in a different home, close by?

WHERE ON EARTH IS MY HOME?

Objective

Geography — To show the children where their homes are in their country and encourage them to think about what is special about their local area.

Group size

Eight to ten children, or larger groups.

What you need

Aerial photographs of Britain and your local area, an overhead projector, large sheets of white paper, sticky tape, thick felt-tipped pens (black, blue, red and green), an outline map of Scotland, Wales, Ireland or the British Isles, paint and brushes (including sponge brushes for variety), easels and bulldog clips (optional).

Preparation

Use sticky tape to fasten your paper together to make one large sheet. Fasten the sheet of paper to the wall at a suitable height, so that the children will be able to reach the part of the map which covers their own locality.

Trace your outline map on to a sheet of acetate using an overhead projector pen, then project the image on to the sheet of paper.

Mix the paint, cut the paper and spread newspaper on any surface likely to be exposed to paint.

What to do

Start by asking the children if they have ever looked out of the window on an aeroplane. Show them the aerial photographs and talk about them.

Sit your group around the overhead projector, so that they can all see the outline of the country they live in projected on to the wall. Explain to the children that this is the shape of their country as they would see it if they were able to fly very high in an aeroplane. Use the felt-tipped pens to draw on the map anything the children think they would see when flying over their locality, such as hills and mountains, rivers and lakes, forests and houses.

Ask the children if they know where their own town or village is on the map of the country. Give each child the opportunity to point out where his or her home is on the map.

Discussion

Talk about the children's home town. What is special about it? How do they remember where it is on the map? Why do they like living there? If they could choose to live anywhere else in the country, where would that be? How far do they go to visit people in the area? Does it take a long time to travel to other places? What directions would they give other people to find the way to their home?

Follow-up activities

✧ Let the children paint a picture of their house (see pages 59–63 for ideas on display).
✧ Ask the children to draw their own map, either of their home or of the room they are in with you. A pair of stepladders in the middle of the room and the opportunity to climb to the top with adult assistance gives a young child the idea of looking at a map from up in the air.

ROOMS IN MY HOME

Objective

Music – To encourage children to develop their ability to distinguish different sounds.

Group size

Up to 30.

What you need

Cassette recorder and a previously-recorded tape, selection of ten musical instruments which make different, easily-identified noises, pictures of rooms in a house, or a doll's house (optional).

Preparation

Record sound-effects of everyday activities which take place in particular rooms in the home. A suggested series is:
1 washing up
2 television
3 snoring
4 cleaning teeth
5 starting up car
6 child playing with friend
7 walking up and down stairs
8 pan sizzling
9 doorbell ringing
10 washing machine
but you can add any others you feel are appropriate.

What to do

Tell the children that you have recorded some sounds of things that happen in different parts of your home. Ask them to listen carefully and then tell you where these things happen in their homes.

Play the cassette and talk about the children's answers. If you have a lot of non-English-speaking children, it would be useful to have some pictures of the rooms in a house, or a doll's house, so that children with limited English language can use gesture instead. Once the children have grasped the idea of a sound representing a place in their home, ask them to choose and play the instrument they think sounds most like a doorbell ringing, a car starting up and so on.

Discussion

Ask the children to be very quiet, as you want them to listen to any sounds they can hear around them. Talk about the sounds you hear. What do they tell you about the place you are in? Are there sounds they only hear at certain times? Are there sounds they only hear in certain places?

Follow-up activities

✧ Make a recording of noises which happen at different times of the day in the room you are in. Ask the children to match instruments to the sounds.
✧ Record them playing their instruments on the cassette recorder.

WINDOWS

* *

Objective

History — To draw an historical scene as if it were viewed from a window in their home.

Group size

Eight to ten, or whole group if required.

What you need

Large sheets of paper, black sugar paper (A2 size), pictures of everyday scenes in the past, paint and palettes, felt-tipped pens or crayons.

Preparation

Cut 5cm-wide strips of black sugar paper down the long side of the A2 sheets. Make sure you have enough to go around the edges of the children's pictures and form a cross in the middle, to make a window outline (as shown below). Put colours in the palettes, if used, and leave a few empty spaces to mix new colours.

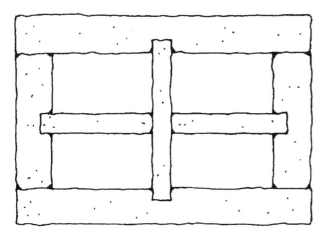

What to do

Ask the children to choose one of the scenes to copy (have a good selection — ragged Victorian children, a wartime scene, a picture showing the exaggerated fashions of the 1970s. Very young children should have just one period selected for them.) Make drawing or painting materials available, and encourage the children to look carefully at the old pictures while making up their own unique interpretations of the painting. Once the paintings are finished and dried, put the black sugar paper

strips around and crossing over them to give the impression of looking out of a window. Sort the paintings into groups which deal with the same period of history, and put them on display boards beneath labels saying:

'What my Mum saw out of her window when she was a little girl';

'What my Grandma saw out of her window when she was a little girl';

'What my Grandma's Grandad saw out of his window when he was a little boy'.

Discussion

Ask the children if they have ever seen pictures or films of how we used to live. Talk about the clothes that people are wearing in the pictures; do we wear the same clothes today? Ask about the transport that can be seen in the pictures — how many cars are there in the Victorian picture? What did people use instead?

Follow-up activities

✧ Dress up as people who lived in one of the periods you have painted/drawn (in the role-play corner).
✧ Ask the children to bring in things from home which date from one of the periods, and display them with the pictures.

WHAT TO USE TO MAKE A HOME

Objective

Technology – To think about suitable materials for building houses and to design a house.

Group size

A group of six children.

What you need

Straw, small twigs, six builder's bricks, two sturdy chairs, the story of 'The three little pigs', a gymnastic mat, paper, pencils.

Preparation

This activity should only be attempted if you are sure that you have enough helpers, and that the children will behave in a sensible fashion! Alternatively, you could use a heavy object, rather than a child, to check the strength of the materials. Place the gym mat down on the floor and put the two chairs close together on the mat, so that a brick can just rest between the two seats. Put the straw, sticks (twigs) and one brick on the floor by the chairs. Read aloud the story of 'The three little pigs', encouraging the children to join in.

What to do

Tell the children that they are going to find out which material is the strongest by checking which will take the weight of a child standing on it.

Put an amount of straw of about the same length and thickness as a brick across the two chairs. Ask for a volunteer to stand on the straw to see if it is strong enough to hold his or her weight. The child should hold the hand of an adult at all times while doing this, as the straw will collapse as soon as a foot is placed on it.

Then put a similar-sized bunch of twigs on to the chairs, and make the same test. This time, the child can put some weight on to the twigs before they collapse. (Hold both hands for this test.)

Lastly, put the brick on the chairs and help the child to stand on it. The children should now be able to recognise which of the three materials is the strongest, and understand why the third little pig's house would not blow down.

Later, or in a new session, find a portion of the grounds where your group can build a small, low wall, using six bricks (see below) and a small bucket of mortar. The children will find this fascinating, and will look at the brickwork of nearby houses in a new light.

Ask the children to design a house, using LEGO bricks. Encourage them to draw their design on paper first, and then see if they can make the model look like their drawing.

Discussion

Let the children touch and feel the straw, the sticks and (carefully) the bricks. What should a building material be like? Should it be strong, waterproof? What was wrong with straw and sticks? Why were bricks better for building a house?

Follow-up activities

✧ Free play with LEGO bricks following this activity helps to develop understanding that the pattern made by the bricks has a purpose in making the structure stronger.

✧ The children can then go on to design and build suitable homes for pet animals, using toys and craft materials. Encourage them to think about the materials they would use for real pet homes, for example metal bars instead of Artstraws.

ASSEMBLE A HOUSE

Objective

PE — To use the process of building a house to provide the structure for a movement lesson.

Group size

A large group (if you have a good supply of helpers).

What you need

A large open space, indoors or outside.

Preparation

If there is a building site nearby, it would be very appropriate to visit it, with the agreement of the site manager and observing suitable safety requirements.

What to do

Once the children are in a large empty space, such as the school hall or an open play area, ask them to stand away from everyone else in a space of their own.

Start by 'digging' the hole for the foundations, bending and stretching as you dig around a circular hole, throwing the earth behind you. Encourage the children to copy your actions. Then think about the concrete to be poured for the foundations. How is it mixed in a concrete-mixer? Roll around on the floor, like concrete being mixed in a mixer, making sure there is plenty of space around each child so that a careless foot does not come into contact with a head. Once the concrete has been mixed, it has to be shovelled into the foundations — time for more shovelling movements.

Now it's time for the bricklayers to start laying bricks and building a wall. Encourage the children to pretend to build a wall around themselves, finally putting the roof over their heads. Next, make the windows and floors by sawing wood and hammering nails. Pretend to carry a large piece of

glass for the windows - this could be done in pairs for older children. Finally the rooms in the house have to be plastered and the walls smoothed carefully.

Once the children have done this at least twice, they could then stretch tall like a block of flats, make themselves low and wide like a bungalow, or float on the river like a houseboat. Then, in pairs, with one child as the car in front and another as the caravan at the back, they could trundle along the roads to live in lots of different places.

Discussion

Talk about the way homes are built. Does anyone know what builders do first when they are building a house? What sort of materials do builders use to build a house? Talk about foundations and concrete, bricks, mortar, wood, tiles and slates. Does the roof go on the house first?

Follow-up activities

✦ Use the photocopiable activity sheet on page 89, asking the children to colour in the pieces of the house, cut them out and assemble them into the shape of a complete house. The house can then be glued into a book or on to a piece of paper.

✦ Say the poem 'Build a house' or the poem 'My little house', both on page 68.

FURNITURE IN MY HOME

Objective

Maths — To sort sets of furniture into the appropriate rooms, developing the key learning strategy of sorting and classifying.

Group size

Six to eight children, or a larger group.

What you need

Sheets of paper, catalogues and magazines with pictures of furniture, doll's house with four rooms, doll's house furniture — at least five items for each room (LEGO house furniture is excellent), small dolls which fit the furniture (LEGO people are fine), adhesive, scissors, crayons.

Preparation

Tear pages with suitable pictures of furniture from the catalogues, so that each child has several to choose from. Ensure that the rooms in the doll's house are empty, and the furniture is arranged where each child can reach it easily.

What to do

Show the children the doll's house. If it is the classic four-roomed cuboid, give each room a name:

Bedroom	Bathroom
Kitchen	Living Room

Ask each child in turn to place a piece of doll's furniture in the appropriate room in the doll's house. Try to get the child to name the piece of furniture and the room they are choosing to place it in.

Make sure that everyone has more than one turn, and try to get all the children to join in the discussion of whether the item has been placed in the right room.

When they have completed the first part of the activity, give each child a piece of paper divided into four to show the rooms of the house. Ask them to cut out and stick appropriate furniture into each room. Very young children may need help with cutting, or may find tearing an easier alternative. They will also find a solid glue stick easier to handle.

Discussion

Talk about the names given to the furniture in the kitchen, bathroom and so on. What is a wardrobe? Do we have a cooker in the bathroom? Do we have a toilet in the kitchen? Where do the children sleep? Where do they keep their clothes? In which room do they watch television?

Follow-up activities

✧ There are several commercial games on the market which can be played in association with the topic of Homes, as well as several jigsaws which show rooms in a house (see recommended materials list on page 96).

✧ The computer program *Albert's House* relates well to this activity. The children use directional keys or a 'mouse' to explore the different rooms in a house which belongs to a small white mouse called Albert.

CHAPTER 2
WHAT HAPPENS AT HOME

This chapter asks children to think about things that happen in their homes, such as having a party, cooking food or wallpapering a room.

GETTING DRESSED

Objective

Maths — To establish a sense of what comes first in a sequence of events, helping young children with their concept of time.

Group size

A group of six to ten children.

What you need

Large table or carpeted area, dolls of either sex and sets of clothes to dress them (one for each child would be best), a set of boy's and girl's clothes, the photocopiable activity sheets on pages 90 and 91, felt-tipped pens, crayons, scissors, *How do I put it on?* by Shigeo Watanabe.

Preparation

Arrange the children's clothes in order from vest, pants and socks, through day clothes to shoes, jacket, hat and scarf.

Put the dolls' clothes in separate piles next to the dolls they fit. Do not put these clothes in any particular order.

What to do

Hold up the items of children's clothing one at a time and ask the group what they are called. Read the story *How do I put it on?*, which shows a small bear who is not at all sure where his clothes are supposed to go. This always provokes amusement, especially when he puts his pants on his head!

Read the story a second time and hold up an item of children's clothing, asking the children how they would put it on. Each child can then dress one of the dolls, hopefully getting the clothes in the right order. Young children sometimes have problems with the dexterity needed for this, so help those whose manual skills are poor; the important thing is to get the items in the right order. Using the activity sheets, encourage the children to choose a paper doll and try to cut it out, together with one of the sets of clothes. The chosen outfit can then be glued to the doll and the whole thing stuck into the child's book. If the children are too young to do this then the cutting should be done by an adult, but the glueing and colouring can still be done by the child.

Discussion

Ask the children how they get dressed. Do they dress themselves or does someone else help them? How many times in a day do they get dressed and undressed? What are the hardest things to put on or take off? Talk about their favourite clothes. What do they like to wear best? Shorts? School uniform? Swimming costume? Do they wear the same clothes at night as they do during the day?

Follow-up activities

✧ Using the dress-dolls from the activity sheets on page 91 as models, ask the children to design an outfit for one of the dolls which they would like to wear themselves.

✧ Older children could design outfits for different purposes such as playing in the snow, swimming in the sea, playing football, or going to a party.

DECORATING

Objective

Art — To help children identify examples of art, craft and design in the home environment. By looking at the patterns on wallpaper and asking children to design their own patterns, this activity also leads to work on Technology.

Group size

Any size.

What you need

A4 pieces of wallpaper of different designs and colours (at least two pieces of each design), squares of cardboard (slightly larger than A4), transparent sticky plastic covering, rolls of lining paper, scissors, ready-mixed paint in saucers or palettes, sponge offcuts or foam printing shapes, pencils, paper, crayons, a can of fixative spray.

Preparation

Make some simple stencils by cutting shapes of leaves, flowers and fruits from thin card. Spray these with fixative spray (available from art and craft shops) to preserve and waterproof them for future use.

Mount the pieces of wallpaper on the cardboard and cover each one with transparent plastic, so that they can be kept clean and re-used for free play.

If using sponge-prints, young children will need pieces of foam already cut into shapes for printing. Older children can cut their own shapes.

What to do

Show the children the pieces of mounted wallpaper. Explain the rules of Pelmanism or 'pairs'. Place the wallpaper 'cards' face down and invite the children to find two cards with the same pattern. Using lengths of lining paper, the children can then design their own wallpaper. Provide young children with ready-cut pieces of foam, and allow older ones to cut out their own shapes, perhaps drawing them first. When the wallpaper designs have dried, they make an interesting display mounted next to each other on the wall like strips of real wallpaper.

Discussion

Talk about the decorating we do in our homes. Who has helped to do some decorating? What is the wallpaper pattern in their bedroom? If the children have brought left-over rolls from home, they could guess which room each pattern was used for.

Follow-up activities

✧ Select a favourite pattern or part of a pattern, and copy it using crayons or felt-tipped pens.
✧ Use a shoebox as a room for the furniture from the doll's house. The children can design wallpaper and carpet for this room.

WASHING THE DISHES

Objective

Science — This activity will allow the children to find out for themselves which washing-up water does the best job of cleaning greasy dishes while they record their observations in simple table form.

Group size

Any size.

What you need

An area where water can be splashed on the floor without causing a disaster — ideally out of doors in warm weather, three plastic bowls of different colours (one with cold and two with warm water), washing-up liquid, plastic dishes (preferably three identical sets of cup, saucer, plate and cutlery), three drainage racks, cooking oil, sponges or cloths, paper divided into three sections, pencils, crayons, felt-tipped pens.

Preparation

Put detergent in just one of the bowls containing warm water, so that you have a progression from cold water with no detergent to warm water with no detergent and finally warm water with detergent. Smear the plastic dishes with cooking oil.

What to do

Show the children that the dishes are sticky and greasy with the oil. Explain that they are going to wash one set of dishes in each bowl to see which water will clean them best. Give each group of children one dirty item and a fixed amount of time

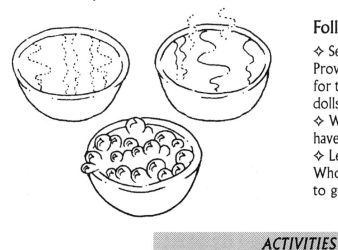

to wash it. When this time is up, leave the items to drain near the bowl in which they were washed. While the dishes are drying, encourage the children to draw three bowls of water, as shown below. They should colour only the one they think got the dishes cleanest. When the dishes are dry, let the children examine them to see if the oil has gone and then decide which bowl of water worked best.

Discussion

Ask the children who washes the dishes in their home. Some may have dishwashers, some may have experience of helping to wash dishes with their parents. Ask the children if they know why we wash dishes (hygiene) and what would happen if we didn't bother.

Follow-up activities

✧ Set up a role-play area outside in warm weather. Provide bowls of warm water and washing powder for the children to have their own laundry for the dolls' clothes.
✧ What is the best way of drying the clothes you have washed?
✧ Learn the poem 'Washing the car' on page 67. Who has helped to wash a car? What did they use to get it clean?

CLOTHES I WEAR

Objective

Maths – To sort the different clothes children have at home and discuss reasons why they are worn.

Group size

Six to ten children, or more.

What you need

Four plastic jointed sorting circles, four blank labels about 20cm by 7cm (label these 'Going to a party', 'Going to school', 'Going on holiday', and 'Going to bed'), paper, crayons, pencils, children's clothes appropriate to the occasions on the labels; a typical selection could be: school uniform (if appropriate), football kit, pyjamas or nightie and dressing gown, swimming costumes, Rainbow or Beaver uniform, party clothes, shorts and T-shirt, wellingtons and a raincoat.

Preparation

Leave the clothes in an easily accessible place, perhaps in a box or bag so that they can remain partly hidden until you wish to show them. Try to ensure that there are some clothes which reflect the multicultural nature of Britain today. Put the plastic sorting circles on the floor with the labels on them.

What to do

Bring out the sets of clothes and encourage the children to discuss where they would wear each outfit. If there is time, some children can be dressed up in the clothes, but do ensure that the girls try on the football kit as well as the boys! Once the child has decided where the clothes would be worn, they can be placed in the appropriate circle. This can be done several times to ensure that everyone has a go!

Discussion

Ask the children why they think they need clothes. Who thinks uniform is a good idea for school? Why do they wear different clothes for different events? Make sure each child gets the chance to listen and to speak.

Follow-up activities

✧ Use different criteria for sorting the clothes, such as indoors/outdoors or winter/summer.
✧ Display the clothes you have sorted (see display ideas on page 62).

PEOPLE WHO LOOK AFTER US AT HOME

Objective

English – To think about and discuss the children's attitudes towards the roles of men and women in the home and to produce a book for the book corner.

Group size

A group of about twelve children.

What you need

A photocopier with an enlargement facility, A4 paper, black felt-tipped pens, pictures of men or women working in the home, a hole-punch and a comb-binder or a coloured lace for holding the book together.

Preparation

Collect a variety of pictures of people working at home – washing dishes, painting, hoovering, gardening, cooking, washing the car, and so on. Photocopy your pictures, enlarging them if necessary to make sure that each fills an A4 sheet. Cut out the people to leave a space big enough for a child's drawing. Photocopy the pictures with spaces, enough copies for each child to have at least one.

Know the background of your group of children. If some children do not have a mum and a dad, vary the words of the poem to suit their circumstances.

What to do

Say this poem:
Here's my Mummy painting the door,
(up-and-down hand movements)
Here's my Daddy hoovering the floor.
(forward-and-back movements)
Here's my Mummy feeding the fishes,
(sprinkle with fingers)
Here's my Daddy washing the dishes.
(rubbing around hand)
Here's my Mummy making tea,
(mime pouring or cooking)
Here's my Daddy cuddling me!
(hug self)

Show the children the pictures and ask them who they think should be able to do the job shown. Ask them to draw themselves doing the job, in the space on the sheet, using the black felt-tipped pens. Allocate a girl and a boy to each sheet. The children can then write 'I can...' and write their names.

Once the pictures have been drawn, punch two holes in the sides and lace or bind the pages together. The book can be left in the book corner for everyone to read.

Discussion

Ask the children if their parents have work to do in the house. Do they do the same work or do they do different things? Talk about the things mums and dads do. Is there anything that Daddy can't do that Mummy can, or vice versa? Is it because they can't or because they don't want to?!

Follow-up activities

✧ Jobs outside the home can be looked at in the same way.
✧ Pictures from magazines can be cut in the same way, and the children can draw coloured pictures of themselves joining in the action.
✧ Consider using the song 'Who's in the garden?' (page 81) with an equal opportunities approach, talking about Mum playing football and Dad making cakes.

HAVING A PARTY

Objective

Drama – To use a powerful situation in a child's life to encourage improvisation and a willingness to participate in an imaginary situation.

Group size

The whole group.

What you need

Party hats, biscuits or fruit, ready-wrapped parcels to play Pass-the-parcel, the song 'Working away' on page 85.

Preparation

Ensure that you have a firm grasp of the story-line. This activity is about improvisation by the children along a path mapped out by you.

What to do

Explain to the children that you will be pretending to have a party. Make a rule, for example, that only the children you point at can speak, but explain that everyone will have their turn.

Story-line

Ask the children to help you get ready for a party – pretend to hoover, then to dust and polish the furniture. Use the song 'Working away' in the resource section, page 85. Next, say that you have to go shopping for the party food, and ask them to come with you to help choose it. Take the children to another part of the room and announce that this is the supermarket. Ask each child to bring you one thing that's nice to eat at a party. You can then mime its preparation.

Once the party is ready, tell the children that you've invited the Gingerbread Man, so someone who knows what he says can have a party hat and come to the party. Give a hat to the first child to say 'Run, run, as fast as you can, you can't catch me, I'm the Gingerbread Man'.

Other characters to invite could be:
the Giant from Jack and the Beanstalk;
the Three Bears (and Goldilocks);
the Three Little Pigs;
the Billy-Goats Gruff.

When everyone has taken on the identity of a guest (use Thunderbirds and other television characters if you run out of ideas), then have some biscuits or pieces of fruit and play Pass-the-parcel, for a real party experience!

Discussion

Ask the children if they have been to a party, or if they've ever had a party of their own. How did they feel at their own party?

Follow-up activities

✧ Write some invitations to a party for other characters, such as Little Bo-Peep, or Cinderella.
✧ Draw a picture of your favourite kind of party (bonfire, birthday, Christmas etc).

COOKING THE DINNER

Objective

English — To talk about favourite food in the home, and provide a reason for writing by asking the children to decide on their favourite meal and describe it.

Group size

Eight to twelve children, or more. Cooking is best done with a small group of four children, with parents to help.

What you need

Plasticine in various colours to make food, paper plates, scissors, adhesive, recipe for a food which is popular with your group. I have used vegetable soup, which is a favourite with the children at our school.

Recipe

1kg chopped vegetables
stock cubes to make 2½l stock
two packets of creamed tomatoes (or similar)
seasoning

Boil the vegetables for ten minutes in about one litre of stock. Purée the softened vegetables (a liquidiser is useful for this), add the stock and creamed tomatoes, then season to taste and simmer for 20-30 minutes until the soup is ready.

Allow the soup to cool before the children taste it. If they are to take portions of soup home with them, you will need to provide some small polystyrene cups with lids.

Preparation

Put the plates on the table with the adhesive, magazines and scissors, making sure that the children have easy access to this work-station.

Check that the children wash their hands before dealing with food, and that the cookery is going to take place in a safe area.

What to do

Decide what to cook, after previous discussion with your group. Talk about the various parts of a meal: starter, main course and pudding or dessert. Make your soup, allowing the children to help with chopping cabbage or other soft vegetables.

While the soup is simmering, encourage the children to create a sculpture of their favourite meal on the paper plates. Make the food from Plasticine or play dough, coating it with PVA adhesive to make it stick to the plate and give it a varnished effect. Ask the children to write labels describing their favourite food and saying why they like it.

Discussion

Ask the children what they enjoy eating at home. Do they know which foods are good for them? Talk about who does the cooking at home. Do both men and women cook? Has anyone helped an adult to make a meal? Did they enjoy doing it?

Follow-up activities

✧ Display the plates on a wallboard or table. Ask the children to assemble complete meals and write menus.
✧ Use the plates of food for use in a role-play corner café.

BEHAVING WELL AND BEHAVING BADLY

Objective

RE – To make the children think about their own behaviour, and the rules that they need to follow.

Group size

Any size.

What you need

Situations to discuss with the children:
1 Chris has painted a really careful picture. He/she has worked on it for a long time, and done his/her very best.
Does Chris deserve a reward or a punishment? Why?
2 Toni sees Chris' picture and when no one is looking, grabs it and rips it to pieces, throwing it in the wastepaper bin.
Does Toni deserve a reward or a punishment? Why?
3 Sam has smacked his/her baby brother and made him cry.
Does Sam deserve a reward or a punishment? Why?
4 Jody has given the little brother a cuddle, wiped his eyes and played a game with him.
Does Jody deserve a reward or a punishment? Why?

Preparation

Your group of children should realise that they must listen as well as speak, that they must not all talk at once, and that they should give everyone a turn to speak. Young children find this very difficult, so consider using a teddy-bear – the rule for this is that only the person holding the teddy-bear is allowed to speak. Care needs to be taken that there are no scuffles over possession!

What to do

Tell the children that you want them to think about behaviour that is good and bad. You want them to decide what rewards and punishments should be given to four children. Read the four situations to your group, one at a time. Children whose families do not operate according to expressed rules can learn from this activity that there are certain forms of behaviour which are encouraged by society, while others are frowned upon. This activity can also be very enlightening for adults, and has been used successfully in a school assembly.

Discussion

Ask about the rules the children follow at home. What happens when they are good? What happens when they are naughty? What would be a really good thing to do for Mum and Dad? What would be the worst thing to do? Does everyone agree that these things are good and bad?

Follow-up activity

Ask the children to suggest some rules which could be used within the group. Write the suggestions on a list and hang this on the wall. Keep pointing it out whenever someone breaks one of the rules, as they surely will!

CHAPTER 3
THINGS WE HAVE AT HOME

This chapter selects a number of objects found in most homes and uses them to provide learning experiences for the children.

KEEPING US WARM

Objective

History – To develop an awareness of the past and of the ways in which it was different from the present, with specific reference to methods of keeping warm.

Group size

Any size.

What you need

Copies of the photocopiable activity sheet on page 92, pencils and crayons, examples of forms of heating used in the past and the present (radiators, electric fires, fan heaters, hot-water bottles, blankets), the poem 'Light the fire!' on page 73.

Preparation

Before you start this activity, see if you can get the heating switched off in your room. If it is winter, this will certainly make an impression on your group!

Have blankets, filled hot-water bottles (warm, not hot, water) and a fan-heater available to help everyone keep warm.

Ensure that you have one copy of the activity sheet for each child, plus a few spares.

What to do

Start by discussing ways of keeping warm which have been around for a long time – open fires, blankets and hot-water bottles. Let each child feel the difference in warmth when they are wrapped in a blanket, and when they hold a hot-water bottle. If the activity is done around November 5th, children may have recent experiences of the heat of bonfires.

Move on to the methods of heating we use today. A fan heater is safer than an electric bar heater, so use the former to warm the room. Let the children feel the radiators while they are cold, then take them to another area where the central heating is still on – can they feel the difference?

Give each child a copy of the activity sheet and ask them to draw circles around the ways of keeping warm which people used long ago.

Discussion

It would be a good learning experience for the children if you could find a pensioner willing to talk about the days before electricity and gas were available. Talk about what people did before they had electric and gas fires. What did cave-dwellers have to keep them warm? What did Grandma have to keep her warm? What keeps us warm today?

Follow-up activities

✧ Anyone working with a small group of children could consider having a very small bonfire in the grounds. Stringent safety precautions must, of course, be taken.

✧ Paint a warm picture and a cold picture – what colours could be used?

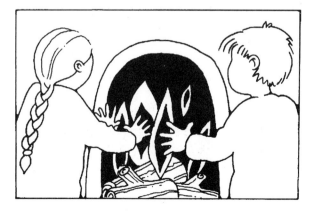

TABLE SETTINGS

* *

Objective

English – To encourage the children's language development by using a common household task as a shared activity and topic for discussion.

Group size

Groups of four to six, to allow each child to take an active part.

What you need

Enough place-settings (preferably brightly coloured plastic) for your group, a photocopier which will photocopy A3 paper, a thick towel or sheet, felt-tipped pens, a table and table-cloth.

Preparation

Put the table-cloth and a small vase of flowers, if you have one, on your table. Place light-coloured (preferably yellow) plastic dishes upside-down on the photocopier in the form of a place-setting. Don't forget the knives and forks. Cover the open lid with your thick towel, and photocopy the dishes and cutlery. Since the place-setting will have to be back to front as well as upside-down to look correct, you may find you need several attempts. One of these photocopies, on A3 paper, can be provided for each child to use.

What to do

On the table place one photocopied sheet for each child. These can then be used as a guide for laying the table. If possible, ask the children to set their own place with a set of one colour, one child finding a set of blue crockery and cutlery while another child finds a red set. After doing this several times, each child can select their favourite set and colour their mat to match it, using the felt-tipped pens.

Discussion

Ask the children about mealtimes at their home. Do they sit down and eat at a table, or do they eat off their laps in front of the television? Talk about the different things needed on the table for a proper meal. What do we use to get the food from our plates to our mouths? Talk about the pleasure of sitting at a table with flowers on it. Ask the children if they've ever been to a restaurant.

Follow-up activities

✧ Set up the role-play corner as a restaurant, with napkins and flowers on the tables.
✧ Provide paper plates and cups and encourage the children to paint or colour them to make sets for the restaurant.

SOAP

Objective

Maths — To use the senses of smell and sight to explore similarities and differences between a selection of soaps, and sort them into sets.

Group size

Six to eight children or as a demonstration for a larger group.

What you need

Lots of bars of soap of different sizes, colours, shapes and scents, sorting circles (collapsible plastic, or large circles cut from paper), blank labels, plastic storage tray, bowl of warm water and a wash cloth.

Preparation

Remove any wrappings from the bars of soap. Put all the bars together in the plastic storage tray. Ensure that there are some soaps with the same colour and some with the same shape. It may be wise to limit the scents to two very different ones, such as lemon and coal-tar.

What to do

Explain to the children that they are going to sort the soaps in different ways. First of all, ask the children to sort the soaps according to their colour. Label the sorting circles with the names of the colours, explaining what the labels are if the children cannot read yet. Once this has been done several times the rule can be changed and the soaps sorted for shape. Once the children have had plenty of experience of sorting using their sight,

explain that they are now going to use their noses to help them sort the soaps. Suggest they close their eyes, so that they are not confused by similarities of colour.

The children can then take turns to wash their hands in the bowl of warm water with one of the bars of soap. While hands are being washed, you can all sing the following to the tune of 'Happy birthday to you':
Wash your dirty hands,
Wash your dirty hands,
Wash them in soap and water,
Wash your dirty hands.

Discussion

Ask the children why we use soap. Is it a good thing to be clean? Where in our homes do we use soap? Talk about the smell of the soaps. What do they think it would taste like? What happens if they get soap in their mouths or eyes?

Follow-up activity

Don't forget to look at the bars of soap again after the children have washed their hands with them. Are they the same size, shape, colour, scent?

A BED

Objective

Maths – To help children develop a sense of the order of events and an understanding that certain things have to be done first for the successful completion of an activity, in this case making a doll's bed.

Group size

Four children, or use this as a demonstration for the whole group.

What you need

Role-play area which is set up as a house, doll's cot with mattress, sheets, pillows and pillowcases, duvet or blankets and coverlet, doll, the poem 'Sea bed' on page 71.

Preparation

Make sure that all the children can see the cot clearly. Place the bedding on the floor, with the mattress on the top and the duvet or coverlet at the bottom.

What to do

Explain that you are going to show the children how to make the doll's bed, so that they can tidy up in the role-play corner when they have finished playing.

Ask the children what they think goes in the cot first. Emphasise that you want them to remember the order in which the bedding goes into the cot, as you are going to ask some of them to do it afterwards. (In a small-group situation, everyone can have a go.) Keep asking the children what they think goes next, and where they think it goes – does the pillow go over or under the mattress?

Talk the children through the sequence as you demonstrate how to make a bed. A suggested sequence could be as follows:
first – mattress
second – bottom sheet
third – pillow (already in pillowcase)
fourth – doll or dolls
fifth – top sheet
sixth – blanket or duvet (already in cover)
seventh – coverlet or eiderdown.

Once the children have seen the cot being made, they can then each have a go.

Discussion

Make sure the children realise that they will be expected to tidy the home corner, and in particular to make the doll's bed if they have been playing with it. Talk about the children's beds at home – what bedding do they have on them: blankets or duvets? Do they have their own bed and their own bedroom? Who makes their bed? How does their bed feel? Read the poem 'Sea bed' on page 71.

Follow-up activities

✧ Children can make their own beds and bedding for small dolls using shoeboxes and scraps of material.
✧ Do some sums with dolls. Put two dolls at the top and one at the bottom of the bed, and ask the children how many dolls are in the bed altogether.

PICTURES IN MY HOME

Objective

Art — To encourage children to look carefully at the paintings found in many homes, and try to reproduce the styles of these works in their own painting.

Group size

Six to eight children.

What you need

Reproductions of paintings, paint in the colours used in the originals, brushes, large sheets of paper (A3), painting aprons, pots of water for cleaning brushes.

Preparation

You may find that children are able to bring in pictures from their home for the group to see. If this is not the case, select some famous painting to discuss with your class. On the topic of Homes, Monet painted the garden of his home many times, and his famous picture of the bridge in his garden may be a good one to ask your children to paint. Matisse's *Red Interior* or *Vincent's Bedroom* by van Gogh could also appeal to younger children. Make sure you have several copies of the same print, and that they are laminated to protect them from accidental paint spillage.

Pour the paint into dishes and spread newspaper or some protective covering over your furniture.

What to do

Show the children the picture they are going to copy. Point out the details they will have to think about: the artist's colours, shapes and method of using paint. Matisse used a flat stylised approach, almost childlike in its simplicity, while Monet used strokes or dots of paint to give an impression of what he saw.

Encourage the children to copy the painting in their own way, drawing their attention to details they may have overlooked, and referring them back to the original when necessary.

When the paintings are finished and dried, they make an attractive display mounted in decorative frames around one of the reproductions, with the artist's name in cut-out letters at the top.

Discussion

Ask the children about the pictures they have in their homes. What are they pictures of? Do they like these pictures? Where are they in their homes?

Follow-up activities

✧ Talk about the colours favoured by famous artists — van Gogh (yellow), Whistler (black and white), Picasso (Blue Period and Pink Period).
✧ Paint a picture in shades of one colour.

POTS AND PANS

Objective

Music – To make musical instruments. The activity concentrates on rhythm instruments, and involves the children in exploring differences of timbre, duration, speed and dynamics.

Group size

Six to ten children (otherwise the noise becomes excessive!)

What you need

Selection of household objects which can be used to make a noise, such as pots, pans, plastic bowls, whisks, spatulas, wooden spoons, plastic hand brushes, graters, rolling-pins, rubber bands of various sizes and instruments which make noises when banged, scraped or plucked, such as drum, guiro, guitar and so on.

Preparation

Put all the household objects (try jumble sales and car boot sales for suitable items) on a table or a clear area of the floor. Put the rubber bands in a container where they can be spread out so that different sizes can be seen easily.

What to do

Ask the children if they think they could use any of the things found in their homes to make a sound. Demonstrate the ways that sounds could be made, using commercially produced instruments, and show them that rubber bands produce sounds if they are stretched across a surface. Then ask the children to use the available household items to make instruments for themselves.

Tell the children that they are going to use their musical instruments to create a rhythm.

First ask the children if they can clap to a beat. Start with their own names, clapping the beats as a group:

—   —   —   —   —   —   —   —

Neil Fenton   Salma Mustafa

Once the children are confident doing this, ask if they can do the same thing with their home-made instruments. Divide them into two groups: strings and percussion! First one group can sound out a rhythm by plucking, then the other group can echo it by tapping or scraping. Once they have done this for a while, try introducing a song which they all know, (such as a nursery rhyme) to see if they can pick up the beat.

To finish, ask them to play their instruments very softly, building up in a crescendo to maximum volume, then fading away again to quietness.

Discussion

Talk about noises we hear in the home. What sort of noises can they hear around them when they are outside their home? What sort of noises do animals make? Can anyone make an animal noise?

Follow-up activities

✧ If the children become very confident, they could sing and play to a round such as *Frère Jacques,* with the two groups taking turns to start.
✧ See how many different sounds each instrument can produce. Can you scrape it, tap it and pluck it? Which sound is the best?

TOYS

* *

Objective

English – To think about favourite toys and to play a game which will test visual memory, using familiar and well-loved toys.

Group size

Six to eight children.

What you need

Small toys, a large tray, a large cloth or a place to hide the tray.

Preparation

Arrange the toys on the tray. These should be brought by the children from home, if possible; but if not, use whatever toys you have available. Try to ensure that the toys you use are all very distinctive, and leave space on the tray between the toys. Make sure all the children can see clearly and are sitting comfortably.

Find a convenient hiding place for the toy you remove from the tray. Place the cloth so that you can reach it easily.

What to do

Explain to the children that you want them to remember all the toys on the tray. Name each of the toys in turn, and point out its position on the tray. Ask the children to close their eyes while you

take one toy away. (Cover the tray with the cloth if there's too much peeking!)

Naming one child, ask him or her to tell you which toy is missing. Give each child in your group a turn, and do not allow the more able to shout out the answer before the rest have had time to think. Do not move the positions of the toys on the tray: replace each in the same place each time.

Discussion

Ask the children about the toys on the tray. What are they called? Where have they come from? Which toy is their favourite? What games can be played with these toys? What toys do they have at home?

Follow-up activities

✧ Let the children make up their own version of the game using different objects – try plastic fruit and vegetables.

✧ Use a felt-board and felt shapes, removing them in the same way and asking the children to remember what was there. Cut your own shapes, or use pre-cut commercially produced shapes.

BUTTONS

Objective

Art — To create a picture using objects commonly found around the home (in this case buttons).

Group size

Six to eight children.

What you need

Lots of buttons of all different colours, shapes and sizes, sheets of sturdy paper or card, PVA adhesive, margarine tubs or yoghurt pots, plastic ties.

Preparation

Collect buttons from any suitable source — cut them off left-over jumble, or ask parents to donate unwanted buttons. Make several different pictures in advance to give the children some ideas of the different shapes they can make with their buttons. Cover each tub in coloured gummed paper to match the contents, then sort your buttons into tubs of colours (the children could do this, as they enjoy it and it is a good basic sorting activity).

What to do

Show your group how loose buttons can be stuck on to card to make a picture. Talk about all the different subjects they could choose to make: a house, an animal, a flower, a car, a train, a person, a robot and so on. Ask each child to put together a picture made from buttons on their sheet of card. While they are doing this, talk to them about what they want their picture to look like. When the children are happy with their pictures, give them some glue so that the buttons can be stuck into their places permanently.

Discussion

Talk about buttons. Where are they found? What are they used for? What shapes do they come in? What colours do they have? What patterns can be made with buttons?

Follow-up activities

✧ Draw round some buttons to make template pictures. The children can then find the buttons which fit the spaces, and remake the picture as a matching exercise.
✧ Take rubbings of buttons to make pictures. Anchor the buttons to the base with Blu-Tack or a similar product.
✧ Print with buttons to make pictures (use plastic ties threaded through the holes and twisted at the back to hold them).

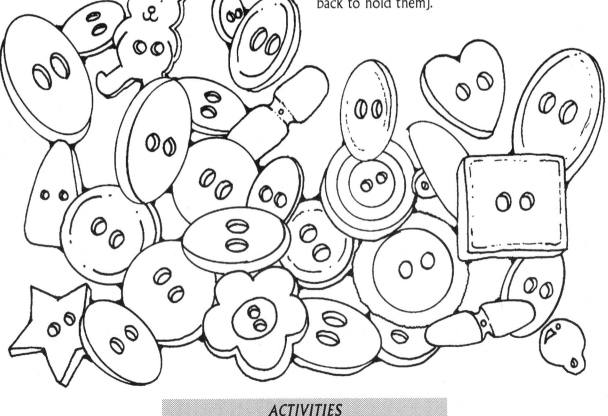

CHAPTER 4
TAKING CARE AT HOME

This chapter invites children to consider what they should do to keep themselves safe and healthy. It includes activities on germs, exercise, healthy eating and taking care of the environment.

MUSICAL GERMS

Objective

Music — To ask the children to create sounds suggested by pictures of germs, and then to compose a short sound-story using the germ-sounds.

Group size

Up to ten.

What you need

Paint, paper, brushes, scissors, pencils, felt-tipped pens, crayons, activity paper in unpleasant colours (bilious green, murky olive or yellow), painting aprons, musical instruments — a different one for each child (car-horns, kazoos, duck-quacks), cassette recorder (optional).

Preparation

Mix the paint. Be sure to include white, as it stands out well against the murky colours of the paper.

Ensure your surfaces are well covered and protected from the inevitable drips.

What to do

Talk about germs with your children — make them aware that germs are unpleasant and often make you sick.

Ask the children to think about what a germ might look like. Then ask them to draw or paint large pictures of germs on the coloured paper. When the paintings are dry (probably the next day), look at them together and choose an instrument to represent each germ.

Very young children need a lot of practice with instruments before they have the control to use them in a structured way. Make sure they have had plenty of experience in free-play situations before you try this activity.

Explain to the children that you are going to hold up one or more of their pictures of germs, and only the instruments matched to those germs should be played. This idea can take a long time to sink in for some children, and you may find that you have to do the activity as far as this several times on separate days before you can take it further. Once the children have got used to watching you holding up the pictures and 'conducting' their 'orchestra', encourage *them* to take turns choosing pictures to hold up and discovering which combinations of pictures make the best sounds.

Discussion

Ask the children if they know about germs. Why is it important to wash our hands after going to the toilet? Are there still germs on our hands after we've washed them? Has anyone in the group ever had a tummy-ache and been sick? Can we see germs? Explain that germs are so small they can only be seen with a microscope. What might a germ look like? What sort of noise might it make?

Follow-up activities

✧ Encourage the children to compose a piece of music about their germs. Record it on cassette.
✧ Ask the children to think about how germs would move to the different sounds. Play the cassette and make up a Dance of the Germs.

SIGNS FOR DANGER

Objective

English – To help children recognise and read signs which warn them of danger.

Group size

Six to ten children or a demonstration activity with a larger group.

What you need

Large card labels with signs for danger on them (see examples below), a photocopier which can enlarge, orange, red, yellow and black felt-tipped pens, the song 'Don't touch' on page 82.

Preparation

Write the word **Danger** in red on one label and photocopy the lightning bolt, the sign for radioactivity, the snarling dog and the product-labels from the illustrations on this page. Use the enlarge facility on the photocopier to make each sign bigger so that the children can see it clearly. A square about 15cm high should be big enough.

Colour the signs, and mount them on to card.

What to do

Sing the song 'Don't touch'.

Show the children the sign with the word **Danger** on it in red. Talk about the meaning of red: red for danger. Read the work together and think about where it could be displayed in the home. Show the children all the other signs, ask them if they know which danger each shows and explain what they mean. Do we have all these dangers in our homes? Think about what we can do to keep safe at all times. Ask the children to make up a list of things to do to keep themselves safe. Record this on a cassette and keep a cassette player in the book corner for the children to listen to whenever they want.

Discussion

Ask the children if they know how to keep themselves safe. How do they know when something is safe to eat or drink? What dangers can they think of that could be found at home? What rules should people have at home to make sure they are safe? What would happen if someone didn't pay attention to signs for danger?

Follow-up activities

✧ Make up a new sign telling people about something that could be dangerous.

✧ Use the activity sheet on page 93 to make a jigsaw of the new sign for danger. Mount it on card and cut around the pieces – then ask other people to put it together. These jigsaws look very attractive mounted on a wall with a bit of space left between the pieces.

HEALTHY EATING

Objective

Science — To encourage children to think about the food they eat at home, emphasising the need for more fresh fruit instead of sweets. To look at what is good and bad for your teeth.

Group size

A large group of children, but with extra adult help.

What you need

Toothbrushes (children could bring their own from home), plastic drinking glasses, plaque disclosing tablets, apples, bananas and oranges (one piece of fruit for each child), unbreakable hand-held mirrors, sweets, shallow dishes or saucers.

Preparation

Lay out toothbrushes and tablets. You will need one toothbrush per child, or per group, and at least one disclosing tablet for each child. Most supermarkets now sell disclosing tablets and toothpaste firms will often provide them free for school projects.

Chop fruit into small pieces, and place on dishes. Unwrap sweets and place on dishes.

Be sure you inform parents that their children will be doing this activity, and will probably be coming home with pink teeth!

What to do

Ask the children if they know what happens to their teeth when they eat. Thanks to television advertisements for toothpaste, children may be familiar with the word 'plaque' and may realise that it is a bad thing.

Use one child as a demonstration, or else ask all the children to scrub their teeth until they think they are clean. Then each child can suck a disclosing tablet. While they are doing this, explain that the tablets will turn any plaque in their mouths bright pink. Then let them look at themselves in the mirrors — this activity causes great amusement because of the pink teeth. Divide your group in two, and give one half some fruit and the other half

sweets. What do their teeth look like now? Which food caused more plaque? Swap over so that everybody has both fruit and sweet, talking about which was better for your teeth each time.

Discussion

Talk about your teeth. Has anyone in the group ever been to the dentist? Was it fun? What happened? Ask the children how often they clean their teeth, and what good they think it does.

Follow-up activities

✧ Make a set of foods good for teeth by printing with fruit and vegetables cut in half.
✧ Make a set of foods bad for teeth by sticking wrappers from sweets, biscuits, cakes and crisps on to a large sheet of paper.
✧ Mount the two sets side by side, with labels to say which is which.

What you need

A large open space (a hall or playground), a cassette recorder, a cassette of suitable music for aerobic exercise, a stethoscope (optional) or some empty yoghurt pots.

Preparation

Set up the cassette recorder and tape – consider using nursery rhymes for young children, as these have a strong rhythm and some are slow, while others are fast.

What to do

Explain that everyone needs to take exercise to keep healthy. Talk about your heart being the pump that pushes the blood around your body. Does anyone know how big a person's heart is? (As big as a fist.) If you have a stethoscope, encourage the children to listen to each others' hearts while they are sitting still (yoghurt pots with the open end held against the chest are fairly effective too).

Go to your exercise area, and let the children check their heartbeats again after each exercise.

EXERCISE IS GOOD FOR YOU

Objective

PE – To think about how hearts and lungs need to work hard to keep healthy, and to develop a short programme of aerobic exercise for children to do every week.

Group size

Groups of about ten children, though the aerobics can be done with a much larger group.

Discussion

Ask the children how they came to the group this morning. Did anybody walk? Ask everyone to stand up and jump up and down energetically for a minute. Can they feel their hearts? Are they beating fast or slow?

Follow-up activity

Give out copies of the activity sheet on page 91 and ask your group to draw the children's hearts, in roughly the right position and roughly the right size.

Suggested routine
Warm-up
✧ bending sideways with hands on hips – 'Mary, Mary, quite contrary' (twice)
✧ stretching up tall and sideways – 'Lavender's blue'
✧ side leg bends – 'Tom, Tom, the piper's son'
Floor
✧ sit with arms back, lifting each leg – 'Jack and Jill'
✧ sit up and lie down with folded arms – 'Hickory dickory dock'

✧ stand and march on the spot – 'The grand old Duke of York'
✧ jogging on the spot – 'Old Mother Hubbard'
✧ star-jumps – 'Twinkle twinkle little star'
✧ kick one leg and clap under it – 'Pease pudding hot'
✧ hopping – 'The north wind doth blow'
✧ walking – 'Baa, baa, black sheep'
Relaxing
✧ lying on the floor on your back – 'I had a little nut tree'

LOOKING AFTER THE WORLD AROUND US

Objective

Science – To think about what we can do to care for our environment.

Group size

Groups of about six children, though this activity can be used as a demonstration with a large group.

What you need

Lots of clean empty crisp packets, sweet-bar wrappers, old newspapers and so on, large sheets of paper, adhesive, black sugar paper, a large area to work on – preferably the floor.

Preparation

Stick the sheets of paper together to form two large sheets about 1.5 metres square.

Cut the black sugar paper into strips. Cut another piece in the shape of a large litter bin.

Take your group outside, preferably around their own homes, and point out litter in gardens or in the street. Provide your group with disposable plastic gloves if you think they will want to pick up anything they see.

What to do

Cut out the shapes of houses from sheets of coloured paper and stick roofs, chimneys, windows and doors on both sheets of paper to create two identical scenes. Trees and flowers could be added by the children.

Encourage the children to stick empty packets and wrappers all over one picture, to make a scene full of litter. Stick lots of litter on the litter bin shape, then stick strips of black sugar paper to look like wire mesh, keeping all the litter safely in the bin. Stick the full litter bin on to the other picture. Encourage the children to talk about what they are doing.

Discussion

Do they find litter around their own homes? Where does this litter come from? Does it look nice? What can we do about it? What harm could it do? What can we do about the litter near our homes?

Follow-up activities

✧ If you can collect litter which is reasonably clean, sort the different types of materials you find. Plastic gloves are essential for this.
✧ What happens to the rubbish from our homes? Where does it go? Find out as much as you can, and invite someone from your local waste-disposal organisation to come and talk to the children.
✧ Ask the children to choose suitable names for the towns shown in the two pictures.

DON'T BURN YOURSELF!

Objective

Art – To think about the dangers of heat and fire, with particular reference to Bonfire Night and fireworks, and to produce some pictures of fireworks.

Group size

Groups of six to eight children.

What you need

Card from old boxes, an old toothbrush and a Plasticine modelling-tool for each child, sheets of black sugar paper, sticky tape or solid glue sticks, Blu-Tack, ready-mixed paint in firework colours, shallow dishes or saucers, painting aprons, a large working area, washing facilities.

Preparation

Cover your working area with newspaper or other protection; include the floor.

Cut out large card silhouettes in the shapes of fireworks, including rectangles, cones and pyramids of varying heights. Make sure they fit on to the middle of your sugar paper, leaving a margin of about 20cm all around them. Pour some of the paint into the saucers (luminous paint is very good for this activity).

What to do

Join the sheets of black sugar paper together to form a long narrow sheet. Ask the children to arrange the firework shapes on the black frieze. When they are satisfied with the arrangement, stick the cardboard shapes to the black background with Blu-Tack. The children can start to spatter paint all around the outlines by dipping the toothbrushes into paint and then scraping their modelling tools across the bristles towards themselves. Once the children have declared their work finished, they can carefully remove the cardboard shapes to find the firework shapes outlined by thousands of specks of colour.

Discussion

Ask the children if they know what happens on November 5th. What do they like best about Bonfire Night? Do they know the names of any fireworks? What could happen to them if they are not careful? Have they ever been burned? Where did it happen? Did it hurt? Where could they burn themselves in their home?

Follow-up activities

✧ Make sets containing drawings or pictures of things that could burn you.
✧ Try to obtain materials and videos produced by the Fire Service to add to the displays on the wall (many local fire services produce information packs).
✧ Ask a member of the Fire Brigade to come and talk to the group about fire safety in the home.

GET ENOUGH SLEEP!

Objective

English – To think about the things which the children do to get ready for bed and to create a book showing what they do.

Group size

Six to eight children.

What you need

Pencils, crayons, felt-tipped pens, paper or card folded in a zigzag (see below) to make a four-page book for each child, a role-play area set up as a bedroom, a cassette recorder.

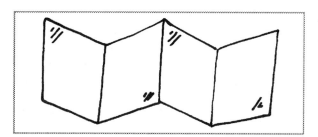

Preparation

Set up your role-play area as a bedroom, with pyjamas and nighties to dress up in, and teddies to cuddle. Include an alarm clock and a book of bedtime stories. Record yourself reading some bedtime stories and, if you feel able, mix in a few lullabies with the stories. Leave the cassette recorder and the tape in the role-play area.

What to do

Do this activity in or near the role-play corner. Adjust the time on the clock to show a suitable bedtime. Ask one of the children to show you how she or he gets ready for and into bed. What happens next? (If the children do not have established routines for going to bed, you may have to suggest that a bedtime story would be a good way of rounding off the day.)

Read one of the stories and sing a lullaby together to the child who is in bed. Explain to the children that when you are not with them in the role-play corner, they can use the cassette instead.

Give the children their zigzag books. Ask them to draw a picture on the first page of what they are usually doing when their mum or dad says that it's time for bed. Ask them to draw themselves washing or cleaning their teeth on the next page. On the third page, ask them to draw someone reading them a bedtime story (this could be you, if they have no other experience to draw upon). On the last page, ask them to draw themselves asleep in bed.

Discussion

Ask the children what time they go to bed in the evening. When do they think their bedtime should be? What do they do to get ready for bed? Do they always clean their teeth? Do they always have a bath? Do they always have supper or a drink? What colour are their night-clothes? Why do we need to sleep?

Follow-up activities

✧ Display the zigzag books on a board near the role-play corner.
✧ Sing the nursery rhyme 'Wee Willie Winkie' and mime the actions.
✧ Read the story 'Strange bumps' on page 74.

DON'T FALL AND HURT YOURSELF

Objective

Drama – To make children more aware of dangerous areas in the home.

Group size

Up to 15 per adult.

What you need

An area to act out the nursery rhyme 'Jack and Jill', a plastic bucket with a handle, a cap and matching hat with plaits attached, brown paper cut into 5cm strips, an empty plastic vinegar shaker.

Preparation

Set up an area as the 'bed' (this could be a rug, mattress or padded bench, for instance) and another area as the 'hill' for Jack and Jill to roll down. A gym mat with a cushion in the middle is quite sufficient and safe.

What to do

Explain to the group that they probably know a song about some children who fell and hurt themselves, and ask them to guess what it is. Then you can all sing 'Jack and Jill' together.

Explain that Jack bumped his head and made it bleed, so Jill bandaged his head with vinegar and brown paper. Then ask for volunteers to play Jack and Jill and wear the hats. Girls or boys can play either part, since the activity is all about playing a part, not playing yourself.

Members of the group now sing the rhyme while Jack and Jill, grasping their pail, climb the hill, mime filling the bucket, fall down, pick themselves up, and go over to the bed. Jack then sits in bed while Jill wraps his head in strips of brown paper, pretending to soak it with vinegar from the vinegar bottle. Make sure everyone has a turn.

Discussion

Ask the children if they have ever bumped themselves or fallen over. How did they feel? After listening to these tales of woe, ask them if they could have done something to stop themselves falling (tidied away their toys so that they didn't fall over them, looked where they were going and not bumped into someone else, and so on).

Follow-up activities

✧ Ask the children to draw a picture of a place in their home where they could fall and hurt themselves.
✧ Use Plasticine or play dough to make a model of Jack and Jill falling down the hill.

CHAPTER 5
PLACES AROUND MY HOME

This chapter looks at the wider community around the children's homes and includes activities involving the church, the post office and the school.

MY SCHOOL

Objective

Geography – To think about the different forms of transport children use to get to nursery or school and make a graph of this information.

Group size

Any size.

What you need

Drawing paper, pencils, felt-tipped pens, crayons, coloured backing paper, adhesive.

Preparation

Decide on the size you want the finished graph to be. Very young children find it difficult to draw on small pieces of paper, so a 10 cm square is recommended. Cut a piece for each child, plus some spares. Stick the backing paper together to make one large sheet.

What to do

Give the children a square of paper each, and ask them to draw a picture of the way they come to the group each morning. Sort the pictures into sets of the same method of transport. Draw an outline for your graph as shown

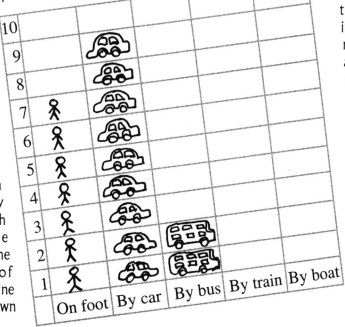

below. Stick the pictures one above the other, in sets. Talk to the children about the information the graph gives them about how they get to nursery or school.

Discuss the totals for each column, and write the numbers at the bottom.

Discussion

Ask the children how they get to nursery or school from home. Why do they travel that way rather than another? Does anyone walk? How long does it take? Do these children live close by? Who travels by bus or car? How long does that take? Do these children live a long distance away? Does anyone come another way? By boat? By horse? How about by aeroplane?

Follow-up activities

✧ Do some addition and subtraction of the totals in the columns. Display these under the children's picture graph.

✧ The children could try to copy the graph into a book (they will need extra help and attention to do this). Squared paper or a ready-made graph photocopied makes this easier, but the activity should really only be attempted with children over the age of five.

✧ The children could make up other graphs, perhaps of favourite toys, using pictures cut from catalogues.

THE POST OFFICE

* *

Objective

English – To develop the children's understanding of what happens when a letter is posted and use the role-play area as a stimulus for writing letters.

Group size

Groups of six children.

What you need

A table or role-play shop-front to be used as a counter, a telephone, rubber-stamps, forms from the Post Office, envelopes, gummed paper or labels cut into stamp-sized pieces, paper-clips, rubber-bands, plastic trays to contain papers, postman's hat, jacket and bag with letters to deliver to members of the group, a post-box, some items for sale, such as birthday cards and stationery.

Preparation

Assemble all the items above. If you wish, you could get your group of children to make the cards for sale, and even make envelopes to fit them if they are capable of this. They could also decorate their 'stamps'. Contact your local sorting office to arrange a visit for your group. Organise an exchange of letters with another group of children in another area.

What to do

Take the children on their visit to the local sorting office. Point out what the staff are doing, so that the children can later model their play on adult behaviour.

Ensure that the children know the rules for their time in the role-play area and let them all spend some time playing in their 'post office'.

Explain that they are going to write letters to children in another place, and that these children will want to know all about them. Young children may find it easier to fill in gaps in a framework, for example:

My name is..................... I like...........................
My hair is...................... I don't like................
My eyes are................... My best friend is.......

Address the envelopes, and take a trip to the nearest post-box to post them.

Discussion

Start off your discussion by singing 'Postman Pat'. Has anyone ever received a letter? (If they say not, mention birthday cards!) Have they ever sent a letter? Why is the address written on the envelope? Does anyone know their postal code?

Follow-up activities

✧ Read *The Jolly Postman* by Allan Ahlberg.
✧ When the letters arrive from your group of pen-pals, let the children read them to each other.
✧ Use G.P.O. resources, such as videos which show the journey of a letter through the postal system. Information and resources are available from post offices, on request.

THE FACTORY

* *

Objective

PE – To get the children to think about factory machines, the different purposes they are used for and the different movements involved. To encourage the children to use their own bodies to produce similar movements.

Group size

30 or more, if there is enough space to move around.

What you need

A large open space or hall, sounds which suggest machinery (percussion instruments, or a cassette).

Preparation

BBC sound-effects recordings make an excellent background to this activity. These may be available from your local library. A video showing factory machines processing food, especially the process of making potato crisps, would be really helpful. Decide on the type of movements you want from the children. Select one sound for each machine. You will need six different sounds.

What to do

Watch the video if you have one. Point out to the children what each machine does. In the open area ask everyone to imagine that they are machines which do one task over and over again in the same way. Ask them to think of a different movement for each machine, and let them listen to the sounds you have selected for each machine.

A suggested preparation could be:
1 a washing machine
2 a peeling machine
3 a slicing machine
4 a frying machine
5 a tumbler for adding flavour
6 a bagging machine.

Once everyone has done this individually, the children could try to link up with children representing other machines in groups of six to make their own assembly line, passing the crisps on to the next machine once they have been processed.

The children could then start to think of suitable movements for the drivers who deliver the potatoes and take the finished products to the shops.

Discussion

Ask the children about other machines in factories. What other foods are made in factories? Does anyone know somebody who works in a factory? What other things can be made in a factory by machines? What can't be made by machines?

Follow-up activities

✧ Design your own packet of crisps, with a new flavour not found in the shops. Design a packet of crisps that a witch, a bear or a worm would enjoy.
✧ Arrange a visit to a factory to look at large machines in operation.

MY FRIEND'S HOUSE

Objective

English – To encourage the children to observe and record things about their friends.

Group size

Groups of six to ten.

What you need

Sheets of drawing paper (A3 size), larger sheets of backing paper (A2 size), crayons, pencils, felt-tipped pens, the song 'My friend's house' on page 83.

Preparation

Try to ensure that each child has enough space to draw and write on their A3 paper without knocking elbows with someone else and without tearing or crumpling their paper.

What to do

Sing the song 'My friend's house'. Ask the children to choose a friend in the group as a partner. You may need to pair some up, or form groups of three. Ask the children to look carefully at their friend in the group. What makes him or her special? What colour is her or his hair, eyes, skin? Let the children draw their friend's face on their A3 piece of paper. Then ask the children to choose just one thing that their friend does that they think shows they are a good friend. School-age children may be able to write this on their own. Others, especially young children, will need help from a supportive adult who could write for them, or help them to copy adult script underneath.

You can then write a group poem or song on the subject of 'My friend's house'. The lines can alternate:

In my friend's house..............................
In my own house..................................

The song or poem should focus on the similarities and differences between the two homes. It can rhyme or not, depending on the age and experience of the children in the group.

For example:

In my friend's house there's lots of chairs
In my own house there's lots of stairs
In my friend's house we watch T.V,
In my own house we stay for tea........and so on.

Fit your words to a known tune *after* it is written. For instance, the above rhyme can be sung to the tune of 'Twinkle twinkle little star.'

Discussion

Who goes to their friend's home? Is it close to your home? Are friends important? Why? How often do you go to your friend's home? Is it the same as your home? What do you like about your friend?

Follow-up activity

Ask the children to draw a picture of their friend's house and a picture of their own house. What is the same? What is different?

THE GARDEN

Objective

Technology — To design and make a miniature garden.

Group size

Six to eight children.

What you need

A4 paper, preferably marked in 2cm squares, seed trays (roughly A4 size), clumps of small rockery plants, Plasticine (green, blue, terracotta), scraps of metallic and transparent blue paper, fine gravel (coloured if possible), twigs, green sponge, brown and green corrugated plastic, scissors, modelling tools, large bag of potting compost, access to a garden area, preferably in the grounds, the song 'Who's in the garden?' on page 81.

Preparation

Take the children for a walk to look at nearby gardens. Point out the differences in the gardens, how some people have lawns, while others have paving stones or tarmac. Some gardens will be well-tended, while others will have grown wild for the birds and the insects. Look at the shapes of the flower beds and the different plants found in them.

What to do

Ask the group of children to draw a plan for a garden that they would like to have at home. Encourage them to think about where they would put trees and flowers, and what shape the lawn or patio would be.

Give each child a piece of squared paper to design a garden, pointing out that a plan is a view as if you were flying over the garden and could see it from above. Very young children will find this difficult, and should be encouraged to draw their design in their own way.

Give each child a seed tray filled with compost and lay out all the materials they need to bring their gardens to life. Split the clumps of rockery plants to form tiny bushes, and show the children how to form miniature trees from twigs and green sponge. Try to ensure that they remember to

follow their drawings. Once the gardens have been planted, and have Plasticine or paper ponds and other features, they will need to be watered regularly to keep the real plants alive.

Discussion

Ask the children what they would do differently if they designed another garden. What did they like best about their garden? What about safety? It might be nice to have fish in your garden, but if there were young children about, would it be safe to have a pond? How could it be made safer? Sing the song 'Who's in the garden?'

Follow-up activity

The children will probably want to take their miniature gardens home, so that the real plants can be planted in their own gardens.

THE CANAL

. . . .

Objective

History – To help the children understand that life was different long ago, and that canals were once an important method of transport for industry.

Group size

Not more than ten children to one adult.

What you need

The opportunity to visit a canal, black wax crayons, 'Brusho' powdered inks (available from artists' suppliers), good quality art paper, brushes of different sizes, pieces of sponge, tissues, old photographs of canals.

Preparation

Contact your Local History Society, and ask if a member would be willing to come and talk to the children before they go on their visit.

Make a visit to the canal before you take your group there, so that you can point out small areas of interest, such as the ridges on the sides of the canal bridges caused by years and years of horse leading-ropes rubbing against the stones.

Discussion

Ask the children what they know about their local canal. Why was it built? Who built it? Who used it long ago? Who uses it now? Ask the children if they know what the boats which go along the canal are called. How do they think they were moved? (Horse and man power, because the wash from steam engines would wear away the clay sides of the canals.)

What to do

Take the children for their visit to the canal. (Parents may be willing to come along as extra helpers.) When you get back to your base give each child a piece of art paper and ask them to draw a picture of the canal in black wax crayon. Suggest they draw their canal across the page, with a definite line between the sky and the land where the canal is. Do they want to draw the canal as it is now, or as it used to be? When the drawings are finished, let the children sponge lightly over the background and foreground in two different 'Brusho' colours. Explain that the wax drawing is not supposed to be covered up by paint, but should show through. Don't let anybody scrub over their crayon with so much paint that the drawing disappears. Pink (sky) and dark blue (land and water) make an attractive, atmospheric 'olde' effect, as do pale lemon and sea-green.

Follow-up activity

Experiment with different combinations of colours, blending them by dabbing with tissues. In this way your sky can be streaked with several colours, giving the effect of sunrise or sunset.

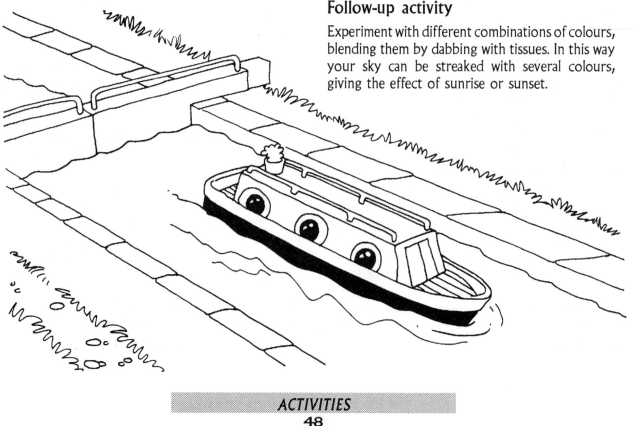

THE CHURCH

Objective

RE – To develop the children's knowledge of their local church, talk about the meaning of the cross and make some decorative crosses.

Group size

Up to 30.

What you need

Photographs or examples of jewelled and decorated crosses or crucifixes, card, beads, sequins, pasta shapes, gold or silver spray paint, PVA liquid adhesive.

Preparation

Contact a local church and arrange for the minister to show a group of children around the church. The minister may even be willing to come to the group and bring some crosses and other items worn as symbols of the ministry. If this is not possible, try to borrow some artefacts from your local teachers' centre.

If you cannot take your group to visit the church, try to visit it yourself, to find out what is there. Some churches provide leaflets which tell visitors the history of the building. If you have religious artefacts, place them where they can be seen, and ensure the children treat them with respect.

Ask the minister to talk about the symbol of the cross and what it means.

Cut out cross-shapes from the card, or allow the children to cut their own if they have proper scissor control.

What to do

If you *are* able to visit a church, take your group and point out that there are lots of crosses used for decoration and on the altar because this is the sign Christians use to show that they believe in Jesus.

Back at your base, give each child either a piece of card or a cross and ask them to decorate it. Pasta shapes look wonderful if they are glued on to the cross and then sprayed gold or silver. If the cross is sprayed first, then beads and sequins can be glued on top, and painted with PVA mixed with water to give a glazed effect.

Discussion

Ask the children about the church near their home. Who is the minister? What sort of objects do you find in a church, and what are they used for? Why do we say prayers, and who do we say them to? What does the cross mean to a Christian?

Follow-up activities

✧ The same procedures can be followed to look at any religion, focusing on a religious artefact and discussing what it is that makes it important to followers of that religion.
✧ The techniques used for making crosses could be used for making jewellery or even Christmas cards.
✧ Effective stained glass windows can be made by tearing Cellophane into strips and sticking these across an outline, as shown below.

strip of cellophane
black paper
this is the wrong side

THE FAST-FOOD SHOP

Objective

Maths – To give the children the chance to learn about buying, selling and giving change in a play situation which will be familiar to them.

Group size

Up to eight.

What you need

Yellow plastic foam sheets, thicker beige plastic foam, polystyrene foam, boxes, napkins, hats (from fast-food shops), empty plastic ketchup bottles, plastic or polystyrene cups with lids, a hole punch, straws, paper coloured in pastel shades, a surface for cutting and assembling the burgers, open-top storage containers, white shirts, green crêpe paper, a till, plastic coins, card, chairs and tables.

Preparation

The children enjoy helping to prepare their fast-food restaurant, so let them make the pretend foods.
✧ Chips are made by cutting the yellow foam into strips.
✧ Burgers can be cut from the polystyrene with a pastry cutter and then painted brown. If PVA glue is added to the paint, it sticks better to the surface.
✧ Burger buns are made from ovals of beige foam cut to take the size of the burgers you have made. Trim these to a bun shape and partly split them, leaving a large amount of join. The top of the bun can be browned with the paint and PVA mix, then, if you choose to sprinkle seeds on the top, they will stick.
✧ Cut up green crêpe paper to make salad.
✧ Stick coloured paper to the outside of the lidded plastic cups as milkshakes. Punch holes in the lids with a hole punch to take the straws.

What to do

Decide on prices for your restaurant, keeping to simple addition of 1p, 2p and 3p. Make a poster and menus showing the price of each article. While children are playing in the home-corner restaurant encourage them to add up bills and give the correct change to customers.

Discussion

Ask the children if they have been to a fast-food restaurant. Is there one near their home? Why did they go? What food did they have? What did it taste like? Who took them there?

Follow-up activities

✧ Do a survey among customers of the home-corner restaurant of what they like about the restaurant and what they would want to change.
✧ Introduce a telephone and a system for booking a table. Design a booking form.

CHAPTER 6
ALL SORTS OF HOMES

This chapter encourages the children to think about a wide range of human homes, as well as homes for animals and characters from fairy-tales.

MY HOME ON THE FARM

Objective

Science – To help children to recognise four farm animals and match them to their homes.

Group size

Six to eight.

What you need

The opportunity to visit a farm (or a toy farm), copies of the activity sheet on page 94, pencils, felt-tipped pens, crayons, the song 'Look around the world' on page 87.

Preparation

Ensure that you have enough copies of the activity sheet on page 94 for each child in your group, with a few spares for mistakes.

Visit the farm yourself before the children, so that you can find the most convenient places for the children to see the animals, and the best animals to see.

Ensure that there are enough adults to supervise the children properly. A ratio of one adult to ten children is normal, although for very young children a ratio of one adult to four children is safer.

If a visit is not possible, a model farm with plastic animals would make a suitable learning aid.

What to do

Take your group to visit the farm, or show them the model. Talk to the children about where the animals live on the farm. Ask them if they know the name of a cow's home (byre) a pig's home (sty) a sheep's home (pen) and a horse's home (stable). If you have a toy farm, name each animal home, ask the children to tell you what the animals that live in it are called, and place them in an appropriate place on the farm. Sing the song 'Look around the world'.

The children should then each take a copy of the activity sheet and draw a line with their pencils to match each animal to its appropriate home on the farm. The sheet can then be coloured by the children, if they wish.

Follow-up activities

✧ Ask the children to paint what they have seen on their visit to the farm. Cut out and display their paintings with posters and photographs showing the same animals. Label each painting 'David's pig', 'Naseem's horse', 'Sofia's sheep', and so on.
✧ Sing 'Old MacDonald had a farm' making all the noises of the animals you have discussed.
✧ Leave the toy farm in the room and encourage free play with all the animals, to give children the opportunity to use the language they have just learned in a relaxed way with their friends.
✧ Find some soft toys of farm animals and design and make suitable homes for them.

FAIRY-TALE HOMES

Objective

Maths – To ask the children to consider the size of different homes found in fairy-tales and to match characters to the right houses.

Group size

Six to ten.

What you need

The photocopiable activity sheet on page 95, felt-tipped pens, crayons, pencils, books of fairy-tales.

Preparation

Ensure you have a copy of the activity sheet for each child in your group, and some extra copies in case of accidents.

Have copies of appropriate fairy-tales to read to the children in case they have no understanding of the size of a giant and a fairy.

What to do

Ask the children if they can think of a very big person, bigger than a house. What would they call a person like that? Has anyone seen one? What sort of home would he live in? What about very small people who can fly and do magic - what do we call them? What sort of homes would they have? Do they know the story of Red Riding Hood? What about Red Riding Hood's Grandma? What size of house would she live in?

Give the children copies of the activity sheet and ask them if they can see a picture of a giant on it. Ask them which of the three homes they think the giant could live in, then ask them to draw a line with their pencil from the giant to his home. Next, ask them if they can see a picture of a fairy, and the fairy's home. Ask them to draw a line from her to her home in the same way. Do the same with Red Riding Hood's Grandma and her home.

The children can then colour in the sheets if they wish and these can be displayed on a wall or in a scrapbook.

Discussion

Ask the children if they know any other fairy-stories. Who reads stories to them? What is their favourite story? What is it about? Can they tell it to the rest of the group? Say the poem 'Who's been sleeping...?' and sing the song 'The three bears' house' on pages 72 and 86.

Follow-up activities

◇ Read the story *The Enchanted Wood* by Gerald Hawksley to introduce the children to other fairy-tale homes.

◇ Ask the children to paint their favourite character from a fairy-tale. Make a large display on the wall with all the children's paintings, putting the names of the fairy-tale characters they have portrayed next to each painting.

DIFFERENT HOMES

Objective

Geography — To help children appreciate the different kinds of homes, temporary and permanent, which exist in this country.

Group size

Six to ten.

What you need

Paint pots, paintbrushes of various thicknesses, including sponge brushes, ready-mixed paint or powder colour in red, blue and yellow (plus black and white), large sheets of paper, painting aprons, palettes or saucers, pictures (preferably photographs) of a variety of homes, including a detached house, a semi-detached house, a terraced house, a houseboat, a caravan, a block of flats, a bungalow and a hostel, the story 'Window in the sky' on page 76 and the poem 'I live up there' on page 73.

Preparation

Try to arrange a walk around the neighbourhood with your group, looking at the different homes in your area. Arrange a visit to a block of flats or an opportunity for the children to have a look around a caravan, so that they have first-hand experience of different homes.

Make sure any work surfaces are well-protected against paint-drips and occasional spills.

What to do

Read the story 'Window in the sky' and the poem 'I live up there'. Talk about the pictures of homes the children are going to paint, making their own colours from the three primary colours on the table. Explain that they are to use just one colour while painting their chosen home, but are to mix two of the primary colours together to make it. Talk about the colours which can be made by mixing yellow and blue (green), red and yellow (orange or brown), and blue and red (purple).

Give each child a palette, and ask what colour each wants to mix. Encourage the children to do this themselves, very carefully, talking them through

the process. Let them choose which type of home they would like to paint, referring to the pictures you have shown them.

Discussion

Start your discussion by asking the children about their own homes, and what sort of house they live in. Use the pictures to show the children types of home they did not see on their walk around their own neighbourhood. Who would like to live in a caravan? Why?

Follow-up activities

◇ Add a small amount of white or black to the paint mixture and ask the child to paint another picture.
◇ Cut out and mount the pictures in sets of various shades of colour.

MY HOME IS LEAVES

Objective

Science – To talk about the hedgehog and its home and to make a hedgehog from leaves.

Group size

Up to ten.

What you need

Lots of clean simple leaves of different sizes and colours, plastic disposable gloves, thin twigs about 20 cm long, brown and black Plasticine.

Preparation

This activity is best done in October, when the leaves are just starting to fall from the trees.

Arrange to take your group of children outside to collect leaves from the trees. Provide plastic disposable gloves so that there is no chance of the children getting dirt on their hands. Make a sample hedgehog to show the children what the finished animal looks like.

What to do

Explain to the children that a hedgehog's home is just a pile of leaves, and that a hedgehog rolls itself in a bed of leaves to hibernate for the winter. Tell the children that they are going to make a hedgehog using the things hedgehogs use to make their home – leaves. Show the children how to push the leaves on to the twig (see below).

Encourage them to start with small leaves, increase the size and then decrease it again, to get a shape roughly like that of a hedgehog. Make a snout from brown Plasticine and stick it on to one end of the stick; make two eyes from black Plasticine and put them on to the snout. A lump of black Plasticine at the other end of the twig stops the leaves falling off, and the hedgehog is complete.

Read the story 'Goodbye, hedgehogs' on page 78 of the resources section.

Discussion

Has anyone ever seen a hedgehog? Where did they see it? What does a hedgehog eat? What could we put out in the garden to feed a hedgehog? Are hedgehogs pets?

Follow-up activities

✧ Let the children search in the library for any books with pictures of hedgehogs, so that you can read them aloud.
✧ Make a hedgehog badge from two shades of thin brown flexible plastic foam, using badge-pins bought from craft shops (see template below).
✧ A large picture of a hedgehog can be made with leaves glued overlapping each other and then painted with a glaze made from PVA adhesive mixed with an equal amount of water. This preserves the leaves and brings out their colours.

MY HOME IS A NEST

Objective

Science – To encourage the children to think about the homes birds make in bushes and trees and to try to make a nest.

Group size

Four to eight.

What you need

Large photographs of birds on nests, small plastic bowls or cups, oddments of wool and hay, a deserted bird's nest (if possible).

Preparation

Cut lengths of wool for the children to use; to avoid problems with tangles, the wool should be rolled into small balls.

What to do

Show your group the photographs and the bird's nest. Ask them to look carefully at how the nest has been woven from all the different materials. Remind them that the bird will have used only its beak to make the nest. Point out the bowl shape of the nest.

Then encourage each child to make a nest. Give them the hay and wool to wind around the bowls until they have made something which looks like a bird's nest. Remove the bowl, leaving the nest on its own.

Discussion

Where do we find nests? Do any other creatures make nests? Was it easy to make a nest? What other things could a nest be made of instead of wool and hay?

Follow-up activities

✧ Display the nests on a table. Can the children make eggs and birds to fit their nests using Plasticine or other modelling materials?
✧ Read the story *The Best Nest* by P.D. Eastman published by Collins.

✧ Try making chocolate nests. Melt one block of chocolate for every 10–15 children (this can be varied, depending on the size of the paper cases you are using). Crumble some cereal into the chocolate and mix well (children enjoy doing this themselves). Spoon the chocolate mixture into paper cases and press the centre down gently with the back of a spoon. When they have cooled down, put three sugar eggs in each nest and ask the children to take them home and show their families before they eat them.

I CARRY MY HOME ON MY BACK

Objective

Science — To supply the children with some facts about a creature they may find in the garden of their home and to make a finger-puppet of a snail.

Group size

Four to six.

What you need

Sturdy card, scissors, felt-tipped pens, crayons, photographs showing enlarged details of snails and their shells, an outdoor area where the children can hunt for snails, plastic containers to keep the snails in for a short time, magnifying glasses or microscopes.

Preparation

Make a template of the snail shell (given below). Six of these templates should fit on to one A4 sheet of card. If more than six are required, photocopy your original on to other sheets of card until you have enough for your group.

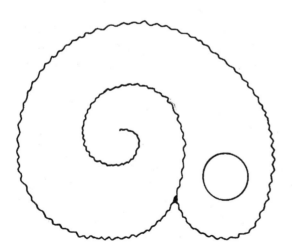

Ensure that snails can be found in the area where you plan to hunt. You can always take snails and put them under the hedge for the children to find, if there are too few around.

What to do

Look at the snails you have found, using the magnifying glasses or the microscope. Ask the children if they could copy the patterns found on the shells, and give them a snail-shell template to draw on. When they have completed their drawings, help them to cut a hole (as shown) for their forefinger. They now have a finger-puppet of a snail, with their own finger acting as the snail's body.

Say this rhyme:
Slowly, slowly creeps the snail,
His home upon his back,
And everywhere he travels,
He leaves a shiny track.

Discussion

Ask the children what the snail's home is called. What words would they use to describe a snail? What happens if you let a snail crawl across your hand? What does it feel like? How can you tell if there are any snails around?

Follow-up activities

✧ Ask the children to use a silver crayon on black paper to make a pattern of snail-tracks.
✧ Can the children move along the floor like snails, very slowly and smoothly? Can they think of a minibeast that moves in a fast and jerky way, the opposite of a snail (a beetle)? Can they think of a minibeast that loops itself along (caterpillar) and one that wriggles (worm)?

MY HOME IS THE SEA

Objective

Art – To encourage children to realise that fish live in the sea and to paint a picture of a fish in the sea.

Group size

Six to eight.

What you need

A (fresh) dead fish, white drawing paper, paint in shades of green and blue or crayons, card, buttons, sequins (optional but very effective), adhesive.

Preparation

Cut out the fish shapes. Older children can do this themselves. For younger children cut out a few different shapes – long thin ones, short fat ones – then children can choose the shape they want to draw around.

What to do

Look at your dead fish and allow the children to touch it. What does it feel like? Point out the scales on the skin of the fish. How would these help a fish to feel at home in the sea? The children should draw around the cardboard fish in the middle of their paper. Younger children can choose a suitable colour and paint a broad stripe all around the outline of their fish. Using a different shade of paint, repeat the stripe around the outside of the previous painted outline. Keep doing this until the edge of the paper is reached. The effect is of a white fish swimming in a wavy sea.

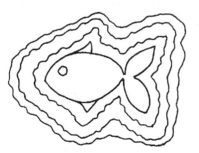

Older children can shade colours from light to dark, or use their crayons to make thick bands of colours around their fish. Let the children stick a button or sequin eye on to their fish. Cut around the edge of the last outline and mount the pictures on the wall.

Discussion

What can you see on the outside of the fish? What do we call the bits which stick out on the top and sides of a fish (gills and fins)? Does the fish smell?

Follow-up activities

✧ Cut your fish open to look at its skeleton.
✧ Bring in a tank of goldfish or tropical fish for the children to watch and talk about.
✧ Similar pictures can be made with other subjects, such as a tadpole, a swan or a starfish. The scope can be extended by using other colours to look like desert (snakes) or beach (shells).
✧ Decorate the cardboard fish shapes and hang them from the ceiling, or use a coat-hanger to make a fish mobile.

MY HOME IS A WEB

Objective

Technology — To inform the children about how a spider catches its food, examine some webs and ask the children to design their own webs.

Group size

Up to six.

What you need

A hedge or railing where there are spiders' webs, A4 paper, fine black felt-tipped pens, clip boards, wool in dark shades (optional), Artstraws or twigs.

Preparation

Search out a hedge or railing with a large population of spiders. Ideally, this would be close by and at a height suitable for young children. Roll your wool into small balls, about 5 cm in diameter. Bind three Artstraws together to make a six-pointed star. Ensure you have one star for every child.

What to do

Take your group to look at spiders' webs. Be careful not to damage them, and try not to let the children poke at them. Look at the spiral pattern the spider has made. Point out that there are long threads supporting the web, which the spider uses to build upon.

Ask the children to look carefully at the spiders' web and draw what they see using the black felt-tipped pens. They will need a clipboard or something else to lean on.

When you are back inside, cut out the drawings and mount them on to a board on the wall.

Older children can weave wool in and out of the Artstraws to make an imitation web. Hang these on the board with the web pictures.

Discussion

Talk about the webs you have seen. Is it easy to make a web? Why does a spider make a web? What would our homes be like if there were no spiders to catch flies? Sing 'Little Miss Muffet' or 'Incy Wincy Spider' with the children. Who is frightened of spiders? Why?

Follow-up activities

✧ A video showing a spider building a web in close-up would be a good aid to language development.

✧ Do some maths with plastic spiders. One big hairy spider and one small spider still makes two spiders altogether. Let the children create their own sums, using two cards with webs drawn on them. They could put the plastic spiders on to the cards, say how many there are altogether, and then write the number if they can.

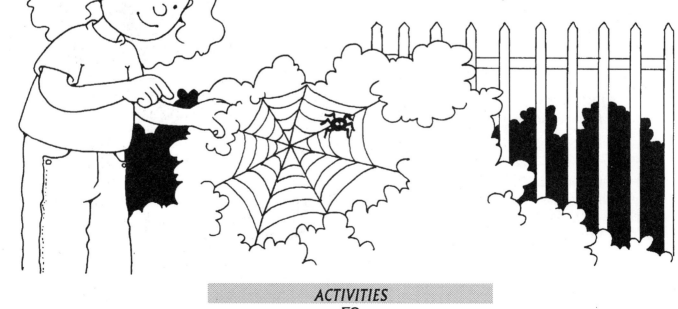

CHAPTER 7
DISPLAYS

Displays of the children's work reinforce learning and provide a colourful focus of interest. The following pages give some general ideas for presentation, followed by more specific notes on two display activities.

IDEAS FOR DISPLAY

Backgrounds

Choice of a suitable background is important in setting the tone for any display. You will obviously have to work with the resources that you have; and while strongly-coloured, single-sided poster paper gives a professional look to a display, it is expensive and may not be available to your group. Whatever paper you have available can always be made more colourful by washing it with a sponge dipped in coloured inks.

Children can also be involved in painting the background. Give each child a sheet of the backing paper, and let them spatter a suitable colour or combination of colours over their sheets. Alternatively, the children could put random patches of glue on to sheets of paper and gently sprinkle powder-paint or sand on to the patches.

Scribbled finger-painting also makes a very good background for displaying children's work. This can be done on newspaper, brown wrapping-paper, wallpaper, whatever you have available.

Outlines

For a display of work on the topic of Homes, paint, draw or cut out the outline of a large house and mount the children's work within it. For other displays, work could be mounted on other large outlines — for example, a hand, a television, a bus, a boat, a tree or a suitcase.

Outlines can also be made with string, coloured raffia, braid, rickrack binding or strips of material.

Frames

Displays look neater and more attractive with a frame around them. For a large display, a strip of contrasting coloured paper around the edge looks effective. Individual children's drawings or paintings look more impressive if they are fastened into an empty picture frame (without glass) using Blu-Tack or something similar.

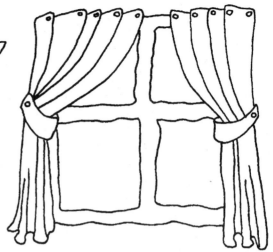

Using texture

Lots of different materials can be used to add interest to your displays. Try using a pair of old brown tights to make a spiky winter tree by cutting it into branching strips, and pulling it tight before fastening it to the display board. All sorts of fabrics make good backgrounds to children's work; they can be used together for contrasting effects, for example velvet and brocade. Why not make false curtains for a display of a window, or consider draping fabric for a display of a bed?

Other materials, such as polystyrene packing, bottle tops, pasta, beads, beans and seeds, can add interest to displays, and can be sprayed with paint in various colours.

Corrugated card, often used for packing, makes a wonderful textured backing to displays. Cut shapes from more of this card and place them on top, twisting the angle of the corrugations slightly in relation to the backing, to achieve a display which looks like an optical illusion.

Interactive displays

Children love books which pop up or move in some way, so seize opportunities to lift flaps and move parts in your displays. The lift-the-flap display mentioned in the activity 'Front doors' on page 11, is an example of this. Instead of finding words under the flaps, young children could find a photograph of the person who painted the picture. Older children could write a riddle, then ask others to guess who painted the picture.

3D displays

There are lots of ways to make displays which have three dimensions. A simple way of adding depth is to fold paper concertina-fashion. This can be used to make leaves for a tree, bird's wings, tadpoles' tails, wriggly worms or snakes, and to add depth to almost any shape which can be cut from a flat piece of paper, including letters and numbers.

A different way of using children's handprints is to mount these on pieces of stiff 'concertina'd' card, so that they move about and appear to wave.

Boxes of all kinds can be useful when preparing 3D displays. Use them to make an actual article, such as a model house, television or lorry, or to support pieces of flat card and make them stick out.

Children's work

Displays of children's drawings and paintings are very appropriate in an early years environment. Leave drawings in their original rectangles of paper, or offer the children circles, triangles and diamonds of paper to see if this influences their choice of subject. Quite often it is possible to enlarge a child's original small drawing by tracing it on to an overhead projector sheet of acetate and then drawing around the image cast on the wall on a large sheet of paper. The children can then colour or paint their large versions.

Paintings should be mounted carefully, sometimes by cutting them along their contours rather than leaving them in their original paper shape.

It is often very effective to mix children's paintings with published material, such as prints of famous paintings on a similar theme, or photographs of animals, people and so on.

Lettering

Lettering used on a display should be appropriate and easily read. Cut large letters from coloured gummed paper. Use large wooden letters which can be drawn around and cut out (see page 96). Hologram paper or card makes very eye-catching lettering for display, as do wrapping paper and corrugated card.

A favourite style of lettering for early years is bubble-writing, where the letters have scalloped outlines and small bubble shapes for any interior spaces.

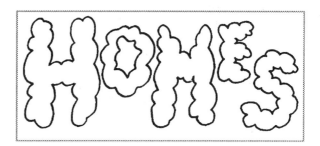

Lettering within displays should always be neatly printed on a label. Consider putting a border around these labels, or cut out clouds from white paper to give them extra definition.

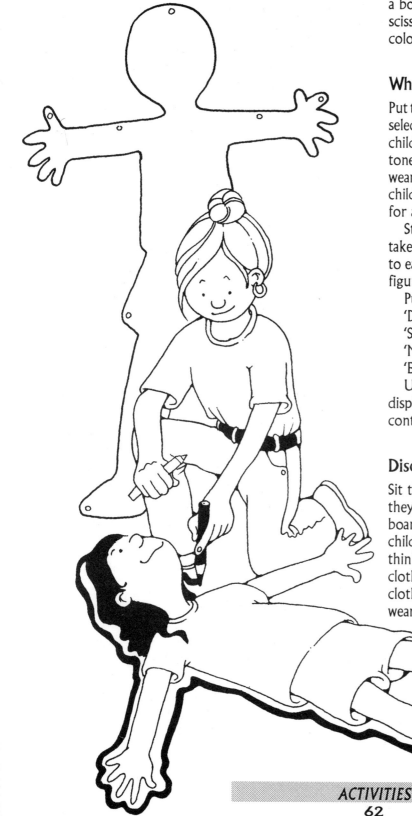

CLOTHES I WEAR

What you need

A display board, a number of different outfits for children (preferably old, or dressing-up clothes), large sheets of coloured display paper (in suitable fleshtones for the children in your group), sheets of backing paper, strips of a contrasting paper for a border around the board, a staple-gun, staples, scissors, a thick felt-tipped pen in a contrasting colour, white paper for 'clouds'.

What to do

Put the backing paper on to your display board and select four children as models. Ask one of the children to lie down on top of an appropriate flesh-toned paper. (This is made easier if the child is wearing shorts and a T-shirt.) Draw around the child and cut out the outline produced. Repeat this for all four children.

Staple the outlines to your display board, then take the outfits you have sorted and staple one on to each outline, as if they were being worn by the figures.

Put labels on the figures, such as:
'David is wearing his football kit.'
'Sajid is wearing his party clothes.'
'Miriam is wearing her pyjamas.'
'Elliot is wearing his jeans.'

Use 'clouds' (see page 61) to put the title of the display along the top of the board. Put the contrasting border around the finished display.

Discussion

Sit the children around the display checking that they can see it clearly. Read what is written on the board, and point out the words, encouraging the children to repeat them. Ask the group what they think the picture children are going to do in the clothes they are wearing. Why do we wear different clothes to do different things? What would they wear to help in the garden, or to wash the car?

ACTIVITIES

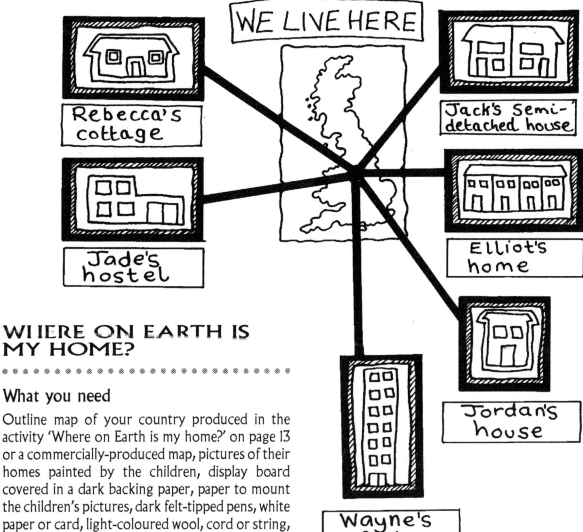

WHERE ON EARTH IS MY HOME?

* *

What you need

Outline map of your country produced in the activity 'Where on Earth is my home?' on page 13 or a commercially-produced map, pictures of their homes painted by the children, display board covered in a dark backing paper, paper to mount the children's pictures, dark felt-tipped pens, white paper or card, light-coloured wool, cord or string, staple-gun, staples.

What to do

Place your large map in the centre of the display and staple it to the board. Mark the location of your town or village by making a large dark dot with a felt-tipped pen. Double-mount the children's paintings around the map. Use one dark and one light colour for the best effect: dark around the edge of the pictures, light around that, as shown below.

Cut lengths of string or cord to join each painting to the dot on the map. Label each painting to say whose home it is. If the cord or string looks untidy where it is stapled to the dot, cover the staple with a circle of dark paper as shown above.

Write 'Where on Earth is my home?' in bubble writing (see above and page 61).

Discussion

Ask the children if they know the name of the place where they live. Can they remember where it is on the map? Use the display to remind the children about the special features of their area. Talk about the names of the towns and cities around the country. Has anyone been to Edinburgh? Belfast? Cardiff? London? Has anyone been on an aeroplane or a boat to a different country?

CHAPTER 8
ASSEMBLIES

This chapter suggests approaches to group sharing-times, which all focus on the Homes theme.

FRIENDS AND RELATIONS

The focus for this approach is on enjoying visits to the homes of our friends or relations, while being glad to return to our own homes afterwards.

The children will be building on their perceptions of their own family life at home and learning to value their experiences as visitors to other homes.

Introduction

The person leading the assembly should invite the children to think about what they value in their own home lives and what they have enjoyed when visiting the homes of friends or relations.

In a small group setting, it will be possible to invite a spontaneous response from the children, but with a larger gathering, it will be more appropriate to have prepared this with children in advance; their suggestions could be given verbally or in another form, such as a mime or role play, or through pictures and drawings.

Activity

The purpose of the activity is to give children an insight into the things they value in their own homes and an appreciation of the enjoyment to be found in the homes of others.

The leader reads or tells the story of 'The Town Mouse and the Country Mouse' (available in various versions from different publishers). Children could act the roles of the characters in the story.

The leader should emphasise how each mouse enjoys new activities and amenities, but is nevertheless glad to be home in familiar surroundings.

Reflection

The leader should encourage the children to think about the meaning of the story, emphasising what the mice liked about staying in a new situation and why they were also glad to go home. These thoughts can be linked with ideas the children have contributed during the introduction.

Prayer

Children may like to be given an opportunity to ask God to bless their own homes and the other homes which they visit.

Song

Children could listen to the song 'Our House' by 'Madness' which has lyrics recalling one person's memory of his home-life.

FAMILY LIFE

The focus for this approach is on the home as a centre for family life and a place which *should* provide emotional security for those who share it.

In this assembly, the children should be able to draw on the activities they have already tackled, particularly the discussions they may have had on 'What makes a home?'. It is likely that these discussions will have emphasised the home as a building, but should also have alerted the pupils to the importance of homes as a place where loved ones can be together in a comfortable and secure environment.

This assembly will work in a variety of settings, with a large group or a smaller gathering.

Introduction

The person leading the assembly should begin by describing his or her ideal or dream home, concentrating on the location, number of rooms and other facilities that might be available, such as a swimming pool or a paddock with a stable block! The children should then be invited to give descriptions of their ideal homes...

In a larger group, it is advisable to ask children to prepare these ideas before the assembly takes place and perhaps record them on paper to read out on the day. In a small group setting, it would be possible to invite more spontaneous comments from the children.

Activity

The leader could give two simple accounts of family life at home which could be acted by children using home-corner equipment.

The first account should show a situation where family relationships are poor – children squabbling over toys, adults arguing about what to watch on television etc.

This should be contrasted with a second short drama showing the same people in the same setting; this time however, they should be kind and supportive to one another, able to relax within the home environment and show that they feel valued and loved. In this scene, family members help one another with domestic tasks and share things.

Children in the audience should now be invited to vote on which of these two homes they prefer; it is hoped that the second will be more popular!

Reflection

The leader should ask the children to consider the reasons why they voted as they did and to focus in particular on the differences between the two scenes.

The children could then be invited to think about what is *really* important in an ideal home and how they can play a part in achieving this within their own home environments.

Prayer

Some children may welcome the opportunity to praise and thank God for their own homes and to ask for help and comfort for those who have no homes or who are unhappy at home.

The prayer might conclude with a request for God's blessing on all homes everywhere.

Song

'Home sweet home' is the obvious choice here, but more contemporary songs may be suitable. 'You've got a friend' focuses on relationships such as one might hope to find in the ideal home.

ALL KINDS OF HOMES

⁕ ⁕

The focus for this approach is on different kinds of homes – houses, flats, bungalows, caravans, hostels and so on. The children gathering for the assembly will be encouraged to be aware of this variety.

Introduction

The leader should begin by explaining that most people have somewhere to live, but they do not all live in the same kind of environment; the children should be invited to think about their own homes and what they are like.

Activity

The leader should now present pictures, models or OHPs of a wide variety of homes, both in this country and abroad, being careful to avoid any stereotypical or potentially misleading examples.

The pictures and models could be produced by the children themselves during previous activities and could include the use of various media and art or craft techniques.

The positive advantages of these different styles of homes could be read out by the leader or announced by the children – bungalows are ideal for people who cannot use stairs, caravans can be moved to new and exciting places, houses usually have a garden, and so on.

Reflection

The children should be given the opportunity to think of the positive aspects of their own homes and to consider how fortunate they are to have a home.

Prayer

Children may wish to join in a prayer; this could offer thanks for different kinds of homes and ask God's help for those who are homeless.

Song

Ralph McTell's song – 'Streets of London' picks up on the homeless theme and could be played to conclude the gathering.

Note: Leaders should always be sensitive to the fact that many children come from unhappy homes which do not provide the material or emotional comforts which are sometimes taken for granted by others.

Collective worship in schools

The assemblies outlined here are suitable for use with children in nurseries and playgroups, but would need to be adapted for use with pupils registered in schools. As a result of legislation enacted in 1944, 1988 and 1993, there are now specific points to be observed when developing a programme of Collective Acts of Worship in a school.

Further guidance will be available from your local SACRE – Standing Advisory Council for RE.

ACTION RHYMES AND POEMS

WASHING THE CAR

*Mime all the actions listed in the poem — sploshing,
washing, soaping, shining, swabbing, rubbing, etc.*
With a Splosh
   Splosh
   Wash Wash Wash
   And a Splosh Splosh Splosh Splosh
   SPLOSH!
You soap soap the bonnet
And you spray spray the door,
You sponge sponge the bumper
And you sweep sweep the floor,
With a Splosh
   Splosh
   Wash Wash Wash
   And a Splosh Splosh Splosh Splosh
   SPLOSH!

With a Rub
   Rub
   Scrub Scrub Scrub
   And a Rub Rub Rub Rub
   RUB!
You shine shine the windows
And you swab swab the wheels.
Hey! *What* a smart car!
And how clean it *feels*!
With a Rub
   Rub
   Scrub Scrub Scrub
   And a Rub Rub Rub Rub
   RUB!

Wes Magee

HERE'S A CUP

Here's a cup, and here's a cup
*(Make circle with thumb and index finger of
one hand; extend arm and repeat)*
And here's a pot of tea.
*(Make fist with one hand and extend thumb
for spout)*
Pour a cup, and pour a cup,
(Tip fist to pour)
And have a drink with me.
(Make drinking movements)

Anon.

MY LITTLE HOUSE

My little house won't stand up straight.
*(Touch fingertips of both hands to form roof and
rock hands from side to side)*
My little house has lost its gate.
(Drop two little fingers)
My little house bends up and down.
(Sway hands)
My little house is the oldest one in town.
(Continue swaying hands)
Here comes the wind – it blows and blows again.
(Blow at hands)
Down falls my little house,
(Hands fall down)
Oh! What a shame.

Trad.

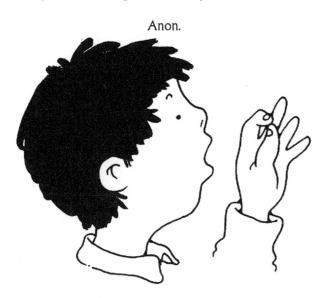

BUILD A HOUSE

Build a house with five bricks,
One, two, three, four, five.
*(Use clenched fists for bricks, putting
one on top of the other five times)*
Put a roof on top
*(Raise both arms above head with
fingers touching)*
And a chimney too,
(Straighten arms)
Where the wind blows through...

WHOO WHOO
(Blow hard or whistle)

Anon.

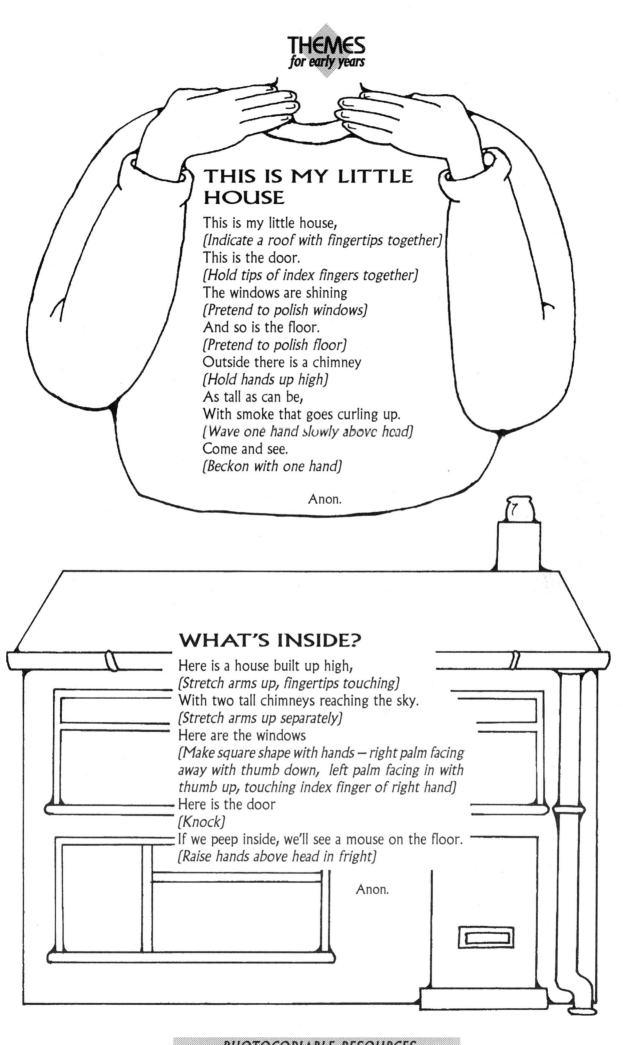

THIS IS MY LITTLE HOUSE

This is my little house,
(Indicate a roof with fingertips together)
This is the door.
(Hold tips of index fingers together)
The windows are shining
(Pretend to polish windows)
And so is the floor.
(Pretend to polish floor)
Outside there is a chimney
(Hold hands up high)
As tall as can be,
With smoke that goes curling up.
(Wave one hand slowly above head)
Come and see.
(Beckon with one hand)

Anon.

WHAT'S INSIDE?

Here is a house built up high,
(Stretch arms up, fingertips touching)
With two tall chimneys reaching the sky.
(Stretch arms up separately)
Here are the windows
(Make square shape with hands – right palm facing away with thumb down, left palm facing in with thumb up, touching index finger of right hand)
Here is the door
(Knock)
If we peep inside, we'll see a mouse on the floor.
(Raise hands above head in fright)

Anon.

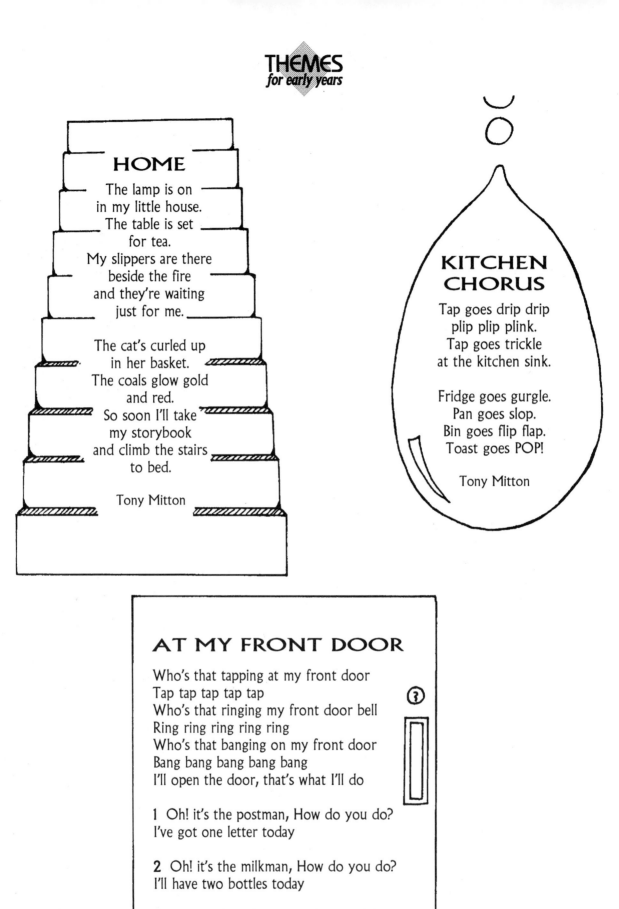

HOME

The lamp is on
in my little house.
The table is set
for tea.
My slippers are there
beside the fire
and they're waiting
just for me.

The cat's curled up
in her basket.
The coals glow gold
and red.
So soon I'll take
my storybook
and climb the stairs
to bed.

Tony Mitton

KITCHEN CHORUS

Tap goes drip drip
plip plip plink.
Tap goes trickle
at the kitchen sink.

Fridge goes gurgle.
Pan goes slop.
Bin goes flip flap.
Toast goes POP!

Tony Mitton

AT MY FRONT DOOR

Who's that tapping at my front door
Tap tap tap tap tap
Who's that ringing my front door bell
Ring ring ring ring ring
Who's that banging on my front door
Bang bang bang bang bang
I'll open the door, that's what I'll do

1 Oh! it's the postman, How do you do?
I've got one letter today

2 Oh! it's the milkman, How do you do?
I'll have two bottles today

3 Oh! it's Grandma, How do you do?
Come in, come in, come in!

Chris Heald

SEA BED

My blue curtains
make it seem to me
that my new bedroom
is under the sea.

Far above the ceiling,
way up there,
I can imagine
boats, birds, air.

But down in my sea bed
I dream and read,
surrounded by fish
and rocks and weed.

Tony Mitton

MY DEN

With a cardboard crate
and an empty sack,
a broken buggy
and a plastic mac,

down in my garden
under a tree,
I've built a home
and it's just for me.

Tony Mitton

MY JUMPER

My jumper
is all
that a jumper
should be.
It's warm
and it's woolly
and friendly
to me.

It's ragged
and fraying
and falling
to bits.
But I can't
throw it out
for it
perfectly
fits.

My jumper
is all
that a jumper
should be.
It's mine
and it's magic
and special
to me.

Tony Mitton

WHO'S BEEN SLEEPING...?

I wonder who owns
this sweet little house
that's tucked so neatly
in the wood?
I'm sure they wouldn't mind
if I peeped inside.
I'll be ever so careful and good.

I wonder who left
these 3 bowls of porridge,
big, medium, small?
The porridge in the small one
tastes just right –
Oh, dear! I've finished it all.

I wonder who sits
in these 3 chairs
that are carved so prettily
from oak?
I think that the littlest one
just fits –
Oh, dear! It slipped and broke.

I wonder who sleeps
in these 3 beds?
The little one seems
just right.
I'm ever so sleepy
and full of porridge,
so I'll just lie down.
Goodnight!

Tony Mitton

EMPTY COTTAGE

Down at the end
of the country lane,
there's an empty cottage
with cracked window panes.

The door's off its hinges.
The roof tiles leak.
The only sounds
are a rustle and creak.

Only the spider,
the slug and the louse
live in the shell
of the old empty house.

Tony Mitton

THE MOUSE IN THE ATTIC

There's a mouse in the attic
Hiding from the cat.
He's made himself a nest
In Mum's old floppy hat.

He wants to be a pop star.
He's written a new song.
He plays it on a banjo
And sings it all night long.

John Foster

I LIVE UP THERE

You see those flats?
I live up there.
Mine's the blue window
Up in the air.

There's lifts and stairs
And doors and doors,
And twenty-seven
Identical floors.

The swings outside
Are too far away,
So we sit up here
With Mum all day.

It's good when it's cold
Up here all warm;
You can watch all the people
Out in the storm.

But if it's sunny and warm outside,
And I'm sick of TV, or I want a ride,
When Dad comes home from the early shift
He takes me down in the silver lift.

Jane Bradley

LIGHT THE FIRE!

Crunch, scrunch,
papers to use;
scrunch, crunch,
yesterday's news!

Criss, cross,
sticks to fix;
cross, criss,
lay those sticks!

Glow, gleam,
black as a mole;
gleam, glow,
beautiful coal!

Scritch, scratch,
ready to light.
Strike the match!
Coal burns bright.

Blaze, burn,
flames leap higher;
burn, blaze,
beautiful fire!

Judith Nicholls

STRANGE BUMPS

Owl was in bed.

'It is time to blow out the candle and go to sleep,' he said with a yawn. Then Owl saw two bumps under the blanket at the bottom of his bed. 'What can those strange bumps be?' asked Owl.

Owl lifted the blanket. He looked down into the bed. All he could see was darkness. Owl tried to sleep but he could not.

'What if those two strange bumps grow bigger and bigger while I am asleep?' said Owl. 'That would not be pleasant.'

Owl moved his right foot up and down. The bump on the right moved up and down.

'One of those bumps is moving!' said Owl.

Owl moved his left foot up and down. The bump on the left moved up and down.

'The other bump is moving!' cried Owl.

Owl pulled all the covers off his bed. The bumps had gone. All Owl could see at the bottom of his bed were his own two feet.

'But now I am cold,' said Owl. 'I will cover myself with the blankets again.'

As soon as he did, he saw the same two bumps.

'Those bumps are back!' shouted Owl. 'Bumps, bumps, bumps! I will never sleep tonight!'

Owl jumped up and down on top of his bed.

'Where are you? What are you?' he cried. With a crash and a bang the bed came falling down.

Owl ran down the stairs. He sat in his chair near the fire.

'I will let those two strange bumps sit on my bed all by themselves,' said Owl. 'Let them grow as big as they wish. I will sleep right here where I am safe.'

And that is what he did.

From *Owl at Home* by Arnold Lobel

Amy was feeling important. 'It's all right, you can leave me here,' she said to her big brother. 'It was ME she wanted to see.'

He waited until Gran opened the door and rode off on his bike.

'Hello, Gran,' said Amy. 'I've come to see your new house.'

Gran smiled. 'I wanted you to be my very first visitor.'

Amy walked inside. It didn't smell like Gran's house - it smelt like her bedroom after it had been painted. The room seemed light and instead of Gran's tiny windows with lots of plants there was only one big one.

'Where are your plants?'

'Plants like special windows. I've left them where they were happy.'

'Where's the picture of Dad and Aunty Grace when they were little? And where's Grandad's rocking chair?'

'They said there was only room for one chair in here. The other one is in the bedroom, come and see.'

Amy had a feeling she wasn't going to like Gran's new home.

'You've only got a little bed, like me.'

'That's all I need,' replied Gran.

Amy sat in the rocking chair, curled up her legs and started to rock.

'It's not right here. It needs to be facing yours.'

'That's just what I thought,' Gran answered, and between them they pushed and pulled until the chair was in the living room.

Soon they were facing each other again. Gran sat in her chair and Amy jumped into Grandad's and started rocking. It still didn't feel right. Then she remembered the picture and went to find it.

While she was in the bedroom she spotted the rug made of rags that used to be between the chairs. She rolled it up and dragged it along.

Gran had her eyes closed, so Amy put the old rug on top of the new one and placed the picture on the sideboard. She settled herself in the chair. She was glad Gran still had the clock because she liked to rock to and fro with the sounds.

'Tick-tock-tick-tock,' to and fro, to and fro and she could see the picture one way and the rug the other.

Gran opened her eyes and noticed the rug and the picture.

'What a clever girl you are, Amy. Let's have some tea.'

'Where's your old kettle?'

'Well that's one thing I didn't mind getting rid of,' she said. 'It took such a long time to boil. Just look at my lovely new electric one.'

'It's just like ours,' Amy said. 'Where's your old one gone?'

'It was an antique,' she replied. 'They paid me a lot of money for it.'

'What's anti... anti...?'

'Antique — means old and precious. There, look, the new one's boiling already.'

Amy was happy to see she still had her special mug, the one Dad used to use.

After tea they sat in the chairs again and Amy said, 'Gran, I do like your new home.'

Gran smiled. 'Yes, I'm liking it better now too.'

Amy was still thinking about the kettle and said, 'Gran — I hope they don't sell you.'

'Sell me?'

'Yes, well you're old and precious, so you must be an antique too!'

Amy could never understand why sometimes Gran seemed to laugh and cry at the same time. All she knew was that she loved her very much.

From *What Shall We Do Today* by Delphine Evans

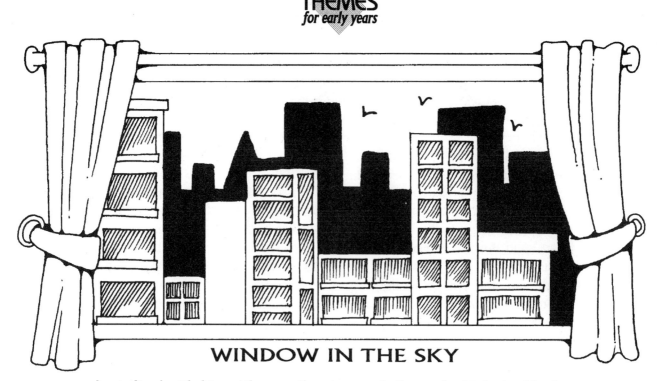

WINDOW IN THE SKY

Jamie lived with his mother on the nineteenth floor of a high-rise block of flats near the city.

From his window he could see the long lines of traffic moving in the streets below. They looked just like toy cars and buses coming and going. There were so many that Jamie was never quick enough to count them all. There must be millions and trillions of cars in the city, he often thought. At night he couldn't see the shapes of the cars, but rows of headlights shining brightly into the darkness told him the roads were still busy.

When the shops far below were lit up with coloured lights, it was like gazing into fairyland.

On the days when there was no smog to lie thick and heavy like a grey blanket over the roof tops, Jamie could see right across the city to the sea. He liked to watch the large ships slowly moving towards the docks, bringing passengers and cargo from the other side of the world. The sea, which looked so calm and flat on a good day, changed into tossing, heaving foam when the weather was bad. It reminded Jamie of the thick, white suds that raced around inside the washing machines at the laundrette.

Sometimes it was a bit frightening living so high up, especially when the wind blew very hard, and the building made strange creaking noises. Often a bird would hit against the window pane with a loud bang.

A friend of Jamie's mother had lent them a telescope, and Jamie loved to watch the workmen on the building sites in the city. They looked so tiny and far away, until he peered through the telescope, and then it was as if the men were inside the room with him.

Sometimes the workmen rode to the top of the building sites on steel girders. They held on tightly, as large cranes slowly pulled the girders higher and higher. Jamie said it would be very handy to have one of those on top of their building, for when the lifts broke down, but his mother said she'd rather walk the nineteen flights of stairs, thank you very much!

Jamie liked watching out of the window much more than he liked doing anything else. His mother was always complaining that he needed to get more fresh air and exercise.

One afternoon, when he arrived home from school, his mother seemed to be very happy. She sang softly as she poured Jamie a glass of milk and put butter and cheese on some biscuits. Then she sat down at the kitchen table and grinned at him.

'I've found a house for us to live in! It's small, and quite old, but it's away from the city, which means you'll have lots of space to run around in. And what's best of all, we'll have a garden of our own. There's even a large tree with a cubby house in it. You have to climb a ladder to get to it.'

Jamie's eyes grew wide with amazement. A house, a garden, and a tree house! He wanted to go, but part of him wanted to stay.

A sea gull, which had strayed too far, leisurely glided past the window.

'Well?' said his mother. 'Aren't you pleased?'

'It sounds terrific,' he said, 'but we won't be able to look out of the window and see the men working on the buildings, or the ships coming and going. I'll feel a little bit sad when we leave this place. Won't you be a bit sad too, Mum?'

'No way!' said his mother. 'I'll always remember the bad things about living here.'

But Jamie looked out of the window and thought, 'Even when I'm sitting in my tree house, in my very own garden, I'm going to remember the good times I've had living way up in the sky.'

By Anita Lucas (from *Big Dipper* ed. by June Epstein et al)

GOODBYE, HEDGEHOGS

The hedgehogs lived in the wooden box for quite a long time. They were called Spike and Spook. Nobody in Class One was quite sure which was which but they all brought things for the hedgehogs to eat. Sharon found snails in her back yard and Ben found slugs and Poppy brought woodlice to school in a matchbox and lots of children brought meat scraps left over from Sunday dinner, so there was always plenty for the hedgehogs on Mondays.

Spike and Spook grew bigger every day. Their prickles were sharp and dark brown by now and if they were frightened they rolled up in a tight ball. But they were both very tame and their eyes were black and shiny as blackberries as they scuttled round their box.

Sometimes Mrs Robinson put on thick gloves and let them scuttle up and down the nature table. But one day one of the hedgehogs fell off the edge of the table. It may have been Spike or it may have been Spook but whichever it was landed on the floor in a prickly ball and then unrolled and ran fast across the classroom floor on little black feet. Some people didn't like it and they jumped on their chairs and squealed.

After that Mrs Robinson said, 'I think it's time we took the hedgehogs back to the park.'

'Oh bother,' said Ben who had found the hedgehogs.

'Oh dear,' sighed Class One.

'Well... hedgehogs are wild creatures and most of them sleep all through the winter.

Spike and Spook are big enough and fat enough to hibernate too, now.' Everyone was still looking rather sad but then Mrs Robinson said, 'We'll all go to the park tomorrow, Friday, and make them a nice hedgehog house to sleep in for the rest of the winter.'

'Oh yes, let's,' said Class One and they cheered up then and that night Sharon made up a poem called 'Goodbye hedgehogs'.

The next afternoon Sharon's mum came to help and Mrs Robinson put the hedgehog box on the rack under baby George's buggy and they set off. Sharon said her poem out loud and Mrs Robinson said it was very nice but really more of a song and after that everybody started singing it:

'Goodbye, hedgehogs, goodbye,
There's plenty in your tummy
And I hope you find your mummy.
Goodbye, hedgehogs, goodbye.'

'We'd better take them back to the place where I found them,' Ben said, and that's what they did.

'How do you make a hedgehog house?' said Harry when they got there.

'First you get lots of sticks and make a pile with a hollow in the middle for the hedgehog to live in and then you pile leaves up all round to keep the house warm,' said Mrs Robinson.

'I'm going to make a hedgehog house right here,' said Ben.

'I'm not,' said Poppy moving a little way away. 'I'm going

to make a hedgehog palace.'

'So am I,' said everybody else.

'Well, don't make too many houses and palaces or the hedgehogs won't know which to choose, will they?' said Mrs Robinson.

All the trees in the park were bare by this time except for the pine trees which had evergreen needles. The paths had been swept but leaves lay all over the grass in rustly yellow heaps. Usually Mrs Robinson said, 'Let the swept-up leaves alone, please.' But this Friday she just watched as everybody got boxes from the litter bin or picked up sticks and made them into little tent things and piled leaves on top.

'Mine is a hedgehog house,' said Ben.

'Mine is a palace,' said Poppy. 'Why don't we make a secret stick passage under the leaves and join them together?'

'All right,' said Ben.

'Me too,' said Harry and Sharon and Charlene and Sam and after that all the hedgehog houses were joined together with secret stick passages and leaves were flying everywhere.

'Hush,' said Mrs Robinson. 'Don't frighten them.' She put on her thick gloves and lifted the hedgehogs out of the box. 'Ready, steady, go,' she said and they both ran straight into Poppy's hedgehog palace and disappeared.

'It's not fair,' said Ben but Mrs Robinson said it didn't matter because all the houses were joined up under the leaves.

'Goodbye, hedgehogs,' said Class One, sadly.

'Goodbye, Spike and Spook,' said Ben.

'Look at those nice cones under the pine trees,' Mrs Robinson said and she began to put them in the old hedgehog box and everybody joined in and soon the box was all full up.

For the first few days people kept forgetting the baby hedgehogs had gone and came to school with a snail or a slug but after a bit everybody remembered. A week later, one cold, wet Friday afternoon, Mrs Robinson put something on her desk and said, 'What's that?'

'Easy-peasy, that's a pine cone,' said Class One but then Mrs Robinson turned the pine cone round and the other end had a face with two shiny eyes.

'It's a hedgehog,' everybody shouted.

'Or a "hedgecone",' said Mrs Robinson. 'And I'm going to show you how to make one.'

She got the box of pine cones out of the cupboard and a box of pins with beady tops for eyes. Some people made hedgecones with red eyes and some people made them with green eyes or black eyes. Charlene found two tiny pearls in the bottom of her pocket from the day Mum broke her necklace and she stuck them on her hedgecone with glue.

The whole box of pine cones was used up and everybody took their hedgecones home. Ben kept his for a long time. That Christmas lots of brothers and sisters found a hedgecone in their stockings and you can still find grannies and aunties in Small Street with hedgecones on their shelves. Some have red eyes, some have green eyes, some have black eyes and just one has tiny shiny eyes like pearls.

From *Winter on Small Street* by Geraldine Kaye

SONGS

IN BED

Jean Gilbert

WHO'S IN THE GARDEN?

Response ▪ or ▪▪ or ▪▪▪ or ▪▪:▪ etc.

Clap

Examples for making up verses:

2 Who's in the garden? Grandma's in the garden.
What is she doing? Doing a bit of weeding.
How many weeds did she pull out?

3 Who's in the kitchen? Dad is in the kitchen.
What is he doing? Making a pot of coffee.
How many cups did he pour out?

4 Who's in the front room? Nicki's in the front room.
What is he doing? Putting all the toys away.
How many toys did he put back?

Jean Gilbert

DON'T TOUCH

1. Our sen-ses are so ve-ry keen, They help us learn so much. But

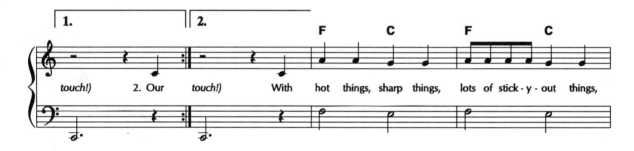

there are times when peo-ple say, "Don't taste, (clap, clap) *don't smell,* (clap, clap) *don't touch!"* (Don't

To Coda ⊕
(last time)

1. *touch!) 2. Our* **2.** *touch!)* With hot things, sharp things, lots of stick-y-out things,

we must do as we're told. And if we do what par-ents say we'll be

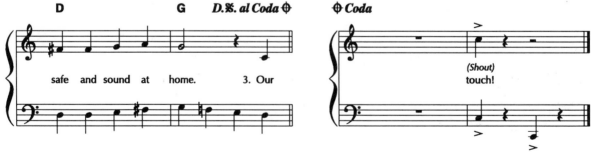

D.℆. al Coda ⊕   ⊕ Coda

safe and sound at home. 3. Our   (Shout) touch!

> **2** Our home's a very special place
> Where we can learn so much,
> But there are times when people say
> 'Don't taste, don't smell, don't touch!'
>
> **3** Our families care for us all
> And love us very much,
> But there are times when they must say
> 'Don't taste, don't smell, don't touch!'

Peter Morrell

MY FRIEND'S HOUSE

My friend's house is bet-ter than mine, 'Cos my friend's mum let's me do what I like. *
Spoken Well, not really.

2 My friend's house is better than ours, 'Cos my friend's
dad lets me play there for hours.
Spoken Well he did once.

3 My friend's house is better by far, 'Cos my friend's sister
has a smashing big car.
Spoken Well, not that big.

4 My friend's house is better you bet, 'Cos my friend's
room is like a zoo full of pets.
Spoken Well there's a gerbil in a cage

5 My friend's house is better by stacks, 'Cos my friend's
brother gives me a ride on his back.
Spoken But he drops me. COME TO THINK OF THAT...

6 My friend's house ISN'T better – no way, 'cos my friend
wants to come to MY HOUSE to play.

Peter Morrell

PHOTOCOPIABLE RESOURCES

AT THE SUPERMARKET
(THE INCREDIBLE FOOD SONG)

Chorus

Sit - ting in a trol - ley at the su - per - mar - ket.__ Look - ing at the dif - ferent things up -

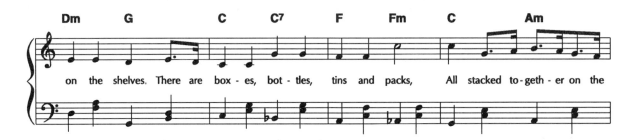

on the shelves. There are box - es, bot - tles, tins and packs, All stacked to - geth - er on the

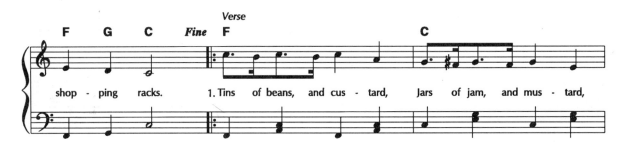

shop - ping racks. 1. Tins of beans, and cus - tard, Jars of jam, and mus - tard,

Verse *Fine*

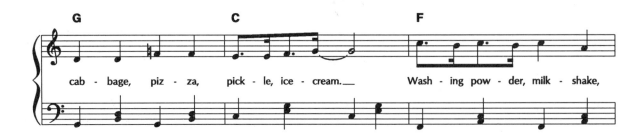

cab - bage, piz - za, pick - le, ice - cream.__ Wash - ing pow - der, milk - shake,

D.C. al Fine

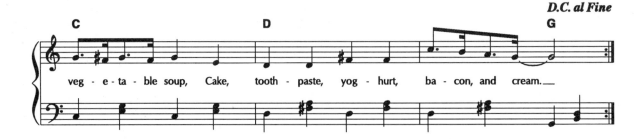

veg - e - ta - ble soup, Cake, tooth - paste, yog - hurt, ba - con, and cream.__

2 Cauliflower, coffee,
Salt and pepper, toffee,
Cat food, jelly,
Curry, shampoo.

3 Fish in batter, sprays and
Treacle, mayonnaise and
Sausage, biscuits,
Marmalade, glue.

Chorus

Achieve incredible foods by not singing the commas in the verses.

Clive Barnwell

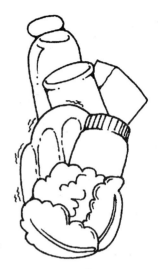

WORKING AWAY

2 Rubbing, rubbing, rubbing away.

3 Sweeping, sweeping, sweeping away.

4 Baking, baking, baking away.

5 Ironing, ironing, ironing away.

Make up other verses and do actions with the words.

Ann Bryant

THE THREE BEARS' HOUSE

The three bears house it looks like this, It looks like this, It looks like this, The three bears house it looks like this in the middle of the wood.

2 The smoke from the chimney curls like this... in the middle of the wood.

3 The flowers in the garden grow...

4 The gate in the garden opens...

5 The water fountain sprays...

6 The trees in the garden sway...

7 The little stream, it runs...
Actions according to words.

Ann Bryant

LOOK AROUND THE WORLD

Look a - round the world,	This is where we live.	Look a - round the
world and you will see,____	Some have homes to live in,	Do you know their
names?	Sing them out,	sing them out with me.____

Fine

D.C. al Fine

Repeat as necessary if sung as a cumulative song

	A	fox	lives	in	an	earth,	that's where it makes its home.
2.	A	bad - ger's	is	a		set,...	
3.	A	hen	lives	in	a	coop,...	
4.	A	cow	pre - fers	a		field,...	
5.	A	pig	lives	in	a	sty,...	
6.	A	bee	lives	in	a	hive,...	
7.	A	spi - der	has	a		web,...	

Continue ad lib.

This song can be taken as a cumulative song, adding one creature each time.

Ian Henderson-Begg

THEMES
for early years

Name _____

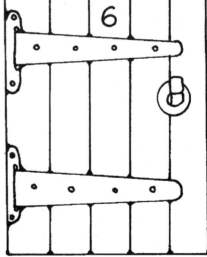

THEMES
for early years

Name _____

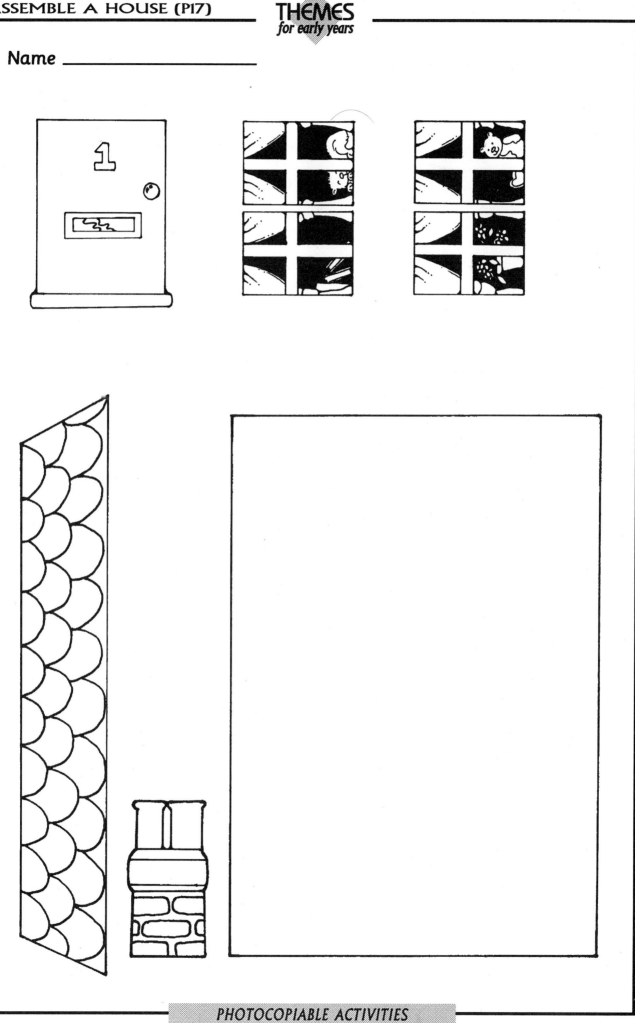

THEMES
for early years

THEMES
for early years

Name _____

THEMES
for early years

Name _____

THEMES
for early years

Name _____

THEMES *for early years*

Name _____

THEMES
for early years

Name _____

RECOMMENDED MATERIALS

BOOKS

Alex's Bed, Mary Dickinson (Hippo Books)
The Bears Who Stayed Indoors, Susanna Gretz (Picture Puffin)
The Best Nest, P.D. Eastman (Collins)
Building Works, Gaynor Chapman (Walker Books)
Bye Bye Baby, Allan and Janet Ahlberg (Little Mammoth)
The Enchanted Wood, Gerald Hawksley (Treehouse Children's Books)
A House is a House for me, Mary Ann Hoberman (Picture Puffin)
How do I put it on? Shigeo Watanabe (Picture Puffin)
I Want a Blue Banana, Joyce and James Dunbar (Dent)
I'm not Sleepy, Susanna Gretz (Black)
Is Anyone Home?, Ron Maris (Picture Puffin)
The Jolly Postman, Allan and Janet Ahlberg (Heinemann)
Ming Lo Moves the Mountain, Arnold Lobel (Walker Books)
Oh Dear!, Rod Campbell (Pan Books)
Peepo!, Allan and Janet Ahlberg (Picture Puffin)
Postman Pat's Washing Day, John Cunliffe (Hippo Books)
Somebody and the Three Blairs, Marilyn Tolhurst (All Books for Children)
There's an Awful Lot of Weirdos in our Neighbourhood!, Colin McNaughton (Walker Books)
This is the Bear and the Picnic Lunch, Sarah Hayes (Walker Books)

GAMES AND PUZZLES

House Floor Puzzle
A 49×68cm floor puzzle with ten large interlocking pieces, plus 12 inset pieces depicting various household objects and activities. From James Galt & Co Ltd, Brookfield Road, Cheadle, Cheshire SK8 2PN (telephone 0161-428 8511)

The House that Jack Built
A matching game from Spears Games, in which children match the colours to build a house. From toyshops or Edco School Supplies, 1 Mallusk Park, Mallusk Road, Newtownabbey, Co. Antrim BT36 8GW or Freepost Leeds LS16 6YY (telephone 0800-243087)

Lift 'n Look House
Puzzle with pieces which can be removed to reveal the different rooms in a house. From NES Arnold, Ludlow Hill Road, West Bridgford, Nottingham NG2 6HD (telephone 0115-945 2200)

OTHER RESOURCES

Letter Templates
Sets of 26 capital or lower case letters to draw around. From James Galt & Co Ltd, Brookfield Road, Cheadle, Cheshire SK8 2PN (telephone 0161-428 8511)

About the House
A set of 160 gummed stamps (70×85mm) depicting familiar objects found in the home, such as sink, cupboard, television and chair. From Philip & Tacey Ltd, North Way, Andover, Hampshire SP10 5BA (telephone 01264-332171)

Lenny the Letter
Resources for teachers about Lenny The Letter, including videos, worksheets, colouring sheets and posters are produced by the Post Office. A catalogue 'Educational Resources from the Post Office', listing prices, is available from the Post Office Education Service, P O Box 145, Sittingbourne, Kent ME10 1NH (telephone 01795-426465)

Albert's House
A computer program where children attempt to get Albert the Mouse past the cat and back into the house. From Rickitt Educational Media, Great Western House, Langport, Somerset TA10 9YU (telephone 01458-253636)